SpringerBriefs in Linguistics

A platform for peer-reviewed short research monographs on all topics in the study of language, including syntax, semantics, philosophy of language, sociolinguistics, psycholinguistics, cognitive linguistics, translation studies, languages and literature, computational linguistics, as well as cross- and interdisciplinary studies in linguistics, and across all schools of thought and all methodologies. Volumes offer concise summaries of cutting-edge research and practical applications across a wide spectrum of fields within linguistics. Compact volumes of 50 to 125 pages cover a range of content from theoretical to experimental and applied research in linguistics. Typical topics might include: • A timely report of state-of-the art analytical techniques • A bridge between new research results published in journal articles and a contextual literature review • A snapshot of a hot or emerging topic • An in-depth case study or fieldwork results • A presentation of core concepts that students must understand in order to make independent contributions. The publishing editor, Christopher Coughlin, welcomes your proposals and ideas for monographs that fit in this series.

Yan Zhang

The Aspect-Sensitive Agent Omission in Mandarin

Springer

Yan Zhang
Jiangsu University
Zhenjiang, China

ISSN 2197-0009 ISSN 2197-0017 (electronic)
SpringerBriefs in Linguistics
ISBN 978-981-96-2986-2 ISBN 978-981-96-2987-9 (eBook)
https://doi.org/10.1007/978-981-96-2987-9

This work was supported by Yan Zhang.

© The Author(s) 2025. This book is an open access publication.

Open Access This book is licensed under the terms of the Creative Commons Attribution-NonCommercial-NoDerivatives 4.0 International License (http://creativecommons.org/licenses/by-nc-nd/4.0/), which permits any noncommercial use, sharing, distribution and reproduction in any medium or format, as long as you give appropriate credit to the original author(s) and the source, provide a link to the Creative Commons license and indicate if you modified the licensed material. You do not have permission under this license to share adapted material derived from this book or parts of it.

The images or other third party material in this book are included in the book's Creative Commons license, unless indicated otherwise in a credit line to the material. If material is not included in the book's Creative Commons license and your intended use is not permitted by statutory regulation or exceeds the permitted use, you will need to obtain permission directly from the copyright holder.

This work is subject to copyright. All commercial rights are reserved by the author(s), whether the whole or part of the material is concerned, specifically the rights of translation, reprinting, reuse of illustrations, recitation, broadcasting, reproduction on microfilms or in any other physical way, and transmission or information storage and retrieval, electronic adaptation, computer software, or by similar or dissimilar methodology now known or hereafter developed. Regarding these commercial rights a non-exclusive license has been granted to the publisher.

The use of general descriptive names, registered names, trademarks, service marks, etc. in this publication does not imply, even in the absence of a specific statement, that such names are exempt from the relevant protective laws and regulations and therefore free for general use.

The publisher, the authors and the editors are safe to assume that the advice and information in this book are believed to be true and accurate at the date of publication. Neither the publisher nor the authors or the editors give a warranty, expressed or implied, with respect to the material contained herein or for any errors or omissions that may have been made. The publisher remains neutral with regard to jurisdictional claims in published maps and institutional affiliations.

This Springer imprint is published by the registered company Springer Nature Singapore Pte Ltd.
The registered company address is: 152 Beach Road, #21-01/04 Gateway East, Singapore 189721, Singapore

If disposing of this product, please recycle the paper.

Contents

1 **Introduction** 1
   References 9

2 **Agent Omission with -*zai*** 11
   2.1 Introduction 11
   2.2 Agent Omission Is Expletivization 15
   2.3 Agent Omission and the M Parameter 22
   2.4 The Aspectual Proper Containment Condition 24
       2.4.1 Agent Omission and Delegation 25
       2.4.2 The Three Tiers of the APCC 32
   2.5 Accounting for the Data with the APCC 33
       2.5.1 1-Phase Verbs 34
       2.5.2 2-Phase Verbs 35
       2.5.3 Examples with Inalienable Possessors 37
       2.5.4 Another Look at the English Data 38
   2.6 Remaining Questions 40
       2.6.1 When Is Delegation Available? 41
       2.6.2 Are Agent Omission Verbs Unaccusatives? 45
   2.7 Conclusion 46
   References 47

3 **Agent Omission with -*zhe*** 49
   3.1 Introduction 49
   3.2 Basic Facts About LoC and -*zhe* 52
       3.2.1 Types of the Locative Inversion Structure 52
       3.2.2 The Definition of -*zhe* 54
       3.2.3 No Implicit Agent with -*zhe* 57
   3.3 Developing the APCC 62
       3.3.1 Agent Omission is Sensitive to Aspect 62
       3.3.2 Agent Omission Is Obligatory 65
   3.4 Accounting for the Data with the APCC 67
       3.4.1 1-Phase Verbs 67

	3.4.2	2-Phase Verbs		72
	3.5	Conclusion		80
	References			80
4	**Agent Omission with -*le***			**83**
	4.1	Introduction		83
	4.2	Discussions on -*le*		85
		4.2.1	The Eventive/Stative Ambiguity of -*le*	85
		4.2.2	A Unified Definition of -*le*	89
		4.2.3	No Implicit Agent with -*le*	93
	4.3	Accounting for the Data with the APCC		99
		4.3.1	1-Phase Verbs	100
		4.3.2	2-Phase Verbs	103
		4.3.3	Evidence from the Pro Drop Cases	111
	4.4	Tan's (1991) Passivisation Account of Agent Omission		114
	4.5	The Difference Between Stative -*zhe* and Stative -*le*		121
	4.6	Conclusion		122
	References			123
5	**Agent Omission with -*guo***			**125**
	5.1	Introduction		125
	5.2	The Definition of -*guo*		126
	5.3	Accounting for the Data with the APCC		132
		5.3.1	1-Phase Verbs	134
		5.3.2	2-phase Verbs	135
		5.3.3	Evidence from the Pro Drop Cases	141
	5.4	Conclusion		143
	References			144
6	**Concluding Remarks**			**145**
	References			148

Abbreviations

APCC	The Aspectual Proper Containment Condition
D	Delegate
DP	Distinguished Phase
EPOT	Ending Point of Time
ExC	The Existential Construction
JVVC	Japanese V-V Compound
LoC	The Locative Construction
PCC	The Proper Containment Condition
RPCC	The Revised Proper Containment Condition
RVC	Resultative Verb Compound
SP	Source Phase
T-DP	Time of Distinguished Phase
TP	Target Phase
Tr	Transitivity
T-SIT	Time of Situation
TT	Topic Time
UEAC	The Underspecified External Argument Condition
VP	Verbal Phrase

Chapter 1
Introduction

Abstract This chapter goes through the research background and raises the two core research questions: (1) what parameter is responsible for the Chinese counterexamples of agent omission to the generalization of UEAC and (2) what rule is the Chinese agent omission subject to. It then briefly introduces the two hypotheses of the work that answers the two questions respectively, and overviews the types of cases that will be later accounted for to give readers an idea of how the core hypothesis captures the phenomenon of agent omission comprehensively.

Keywords The causative/unaccusative alternation · Agent omission in Mandarin · Aspect

The causative/unaccusative alternation, as exemplified in (1), has been widely found and studied cross-linguistically. In (1a), the verb *break* has a transitive form that takes both an external argument and an internal argument, while in (1b) it is in an unaccusative form and projects an internal argument only.

(1)   a. John broke the window.
        b. The window broke.

This alternation is not compatible with every verb in English, however. For example, the transitive verb *install* does not allow an unaccusative counterpart, which is shown in (2a)/(2b).

(2)   a. John installed the air-conditioner.
        b. *The air-conditioner installed.

The contrast reflected in (1) and (2) is widely found cross-linguistically, and a condition has been formulated to account for this contrast: to allow the alternation, a

---

This monograph was an adapted version of the same author's Ph.D. dissertation titled "No loitering: on the omission of external arguments in Mandarin Chinese". The dissertation was submitted to University College London in 2022. The copyright of the dissertation belongs to the author (Zhang 2022).

verb has to be unselective in its external argument, i.e., either agent, instrument or causer must be allowed as the external argument (Levin and Rappaport Hovav 1995; Reinhart 2002; Alexiadou et al. 2015). For example, *break* allows either an agent, an instrument or a cause to be its external argument and thus is unselective, while *install* is selective and requires an agent. It is therefore predicted that (1b) is felicitous while (2b) is not. The above condition is referred to as the *Underspecified External Argument Condition* (UEAC) by Alexiadou et al. (2015).

A core prediction of the UEAC is that an external argument specified by the predicate as [+m] (i.e., an argument whose mental state is implicated in the event denoted by the predicate) can never be omitted. In other words, a predicate that necessarily selects an agent is predicted to be incompatible with an agentless variant in any language. However, potential counterexamples are unexpectedly found in Mandarin Chinese. Examples are given in (3).

(3) a. Lisi zai anzhuang kongtiao.
    Lisi ASP install air-conditioner
    i) 'Lisi is installing the air-conditioner.'
    ii) 'Lisi is having someone install the air-conditioner.'
  b. Kongtiao zai anzhuang.
    air-conditioner ASP install
    'The air-conditioner is being installed.'

I will show in the coming chapters that the agent in (3b) is thoroughly removed (i.e., expletivized) rather than covertly present, so that such data are indeed a challenge to the UEAC. This then raises the question whether it is possible to account for these counterexamples without denying the UEAC as a valid cross-linguistic generalisation. Is there a parameter that captures this contrast between Chinese and English (as well as numerous other languages), and if there is, what is this parameter?

These questions are not the only questions we are facing when considering these agent omission cases. Apart from the fact that we must determine what allows the agent to be omitted in Chinese, there is also evidence that agent omission is subject to restrictions. For example, agent omission is not allowed in (4).

(4) a. Lisi zai da Zhangsan.
    Lisi ASP hit Zhangsan
    i) 'Lisi is hitting Zhangsan.'
    ii) *'Lisi is having someone hit Zhangsan.'
  b. *Zhangsan zai da.
    Zhangsan ASP hit
    Intended meaning: 'Zhangsan is being hit.'

1 Introduction

In this monograph, I will propose and defend two hypotheses. The first concerns the nature of a parameter that allows Chinese to have agent omission in cases where this is disallowed in English. The second, concerns the circumstances in which agent omission in Chinese is blocked.

As I have shown above, the UEAC, or at least its core property, is expected to hold cross-linguistically. Therefore, the agent omission cases in Mandarin Chinese are surprising. Considering that the UEAC makes correct predictions in many languages but not Chinese, one potential account could be that different settings of a particular parameter leads to this contrast. In other words, the condition that an agent cannot be removed if it is required by the verb only applies to the languages that have one setting of this parameter, but not to languages that have the other. English (and Dutch, German, as well as many other languages) belongs to the former camp while Chinese belongs to the latter one.

If this idea makes sense, the next question is what exactly this parameter is, and to answer this question, we need to consider why being selected by the verb can block the elimination of an agent. In this respect, I follow the hypothesis put forward by Reinhart (2002) and assume that expletivization of the external argument is blocked if this argument is specified as [+m], that is as possessing a mental state. This feature can be considered a grammaticalization of a semantic property encoded in the verb. In particular, verbs that select the [+m] feature on their external argument contain a manner component or a result component associated with actions by an individual with a mental state. Selection for the [+m] feature entails that the external argument cannot be interpreted as a pure cause or as an instrument, since neither of these have mental states and therefore either lack the [+m] feature or carry a negative specification for it.

We can capture the difference between English and similar languages on the one hand and Chinese and similar languages on the other by postulating that only the former group grammaticalizes the presence of an actor with a mental state in the verbal concept through the [+m] feature. Because in these languages, the requirement for [+m] is encoded syntactically in the predicate, the relevant verbs are "selective" and display sensitivity to the UEAC. By contrast, the [+m] feature is systematically absent in Mandarin Chinese. That is to say, different from English, a Chinese agentive verb does not encode the presence of an agent in the verbal concept through a grammatical feature. Of course, a context that supports these agent entailments will be required by the relevant semantics in Chinese, but this is not a non-negotiable grammatical requirement. Chinese thus allows the [+m] external arguments to be omitted. At the same time, it also permits the external argument—when present—to be interpreted as a delegator rather than as the agent carrying out the action specified by the verb. The availability of delegation readings plays a significant role in my later analysis.

(5)   a.   Lisi   zai   anzhuang   kongtiao.

	Lisi	ASP	install	air-conditioner

  i) 'Lisi is installing the air-conditioner.'
  ii) 'Lisi is having someone install the air-conditioner.'

b. Lisi is installing the air-conditioner.
(Lisi must be the person who does the installing action)

Thus, the parameter that captures the contrast between Chinese and English is whether an agentive verb selects a [+m] feature on its external argument. I have named this the M parameter. The M parameter explains why the UEAC is a cross-linguistic condition but does not apply to Chinese.

We then come to the question of how we should account for the fact that agent omission is not always available. The M parameter already determines that there is no grammatical restriction in Mandarin: since no external argument is marked [+m], expletivization is generally available. So what distinguishes the possible from the impossible cases of agent omission? A hint at what sort of constraint might be needed comes from the observation that agent omission is systematically permitted in contexts of delegation. For example, (3a) permits a delegation reading and supports agent omission (see (3b)), while (4a) does not allow a delegation reading and also does not support agent omission (see (4b)). Moreover, some agent omission examples sound bad when uttered out of the blue, but become a lot more acceptable when a delegation context is provided, as demonstrated by the contrast in (6).

(6) a. (Context: a customer is buying books)

*Shu	zai	mai.
book	ASP	buy

b. (Context: the library of my university is purchasing a book for which I requested a loan. When I ask whether it has arrived, the librarian says, 'please bear with us…*shu zai mai*.')

Shu	zai	mai
book	ASP	buy

Why does this association between delegation and omission exist and what does it reflect? A sensible conjecture can be that a delegation context is one in which an external argument does not need to 'do something' in the eventuality denoted by the verb: it could be this property of the argument that makes it eligible for omission. This idea has affinity with the Proper Containment Condition (PCC) proposed by Rappaport Hovav and Levin (2012), a contextual constraint on the causative alternation.

1 Introduction

(7) The Proper Containment Condition: When a change of state is properly contained within a causing act, the argument representing that act must be expressed in the same clause as the verb describing the change of state.
(Rappaport Hovav and Levin 2012, 173)

The PCC was proposed to account for the fact that verbs that are unselective in their external argument do not support expletivization in every context. For example, it captures the contrast in (8): the causing act performed by the waiter is properly contained in the change of state of the counter from not clear to clear, and so expletivization is blocked.

(8) a. The waiter cleared the counter.
     b. *The counter cleared. (Rappaport Hovav and Levin 2012, 172)

The PCC could be said to allow one to do away with Reinhart's condition on expletivization (namely that the operation is blocked if the verb selects a [+m] argument). This is because a verb that selects a [+m] external argument contains a manner component or a result component associated with actions by the referent of that external argument. Therefore, expletivization of the external argument of a verb is guaranteed to violate the PCC.

However, the Chinese setting for the M parameter entails that the external argument of, say, a manner verb does not have to be associated with the event of which the manner verb specifies the manner. Such a verb semantically encodes that it involves a particular activity, but it does not specify that its external argument is a participant in that activity. It is this aspect of Chinese manner verbs that makes them compatible with interpretations of delegation.

It is easy to see that the intuition expressed by the PCC is very relevant to the Chinese data: in our mental model the actions of a delegator do not overlap with the event of change, because the delegator is not a participant in that event. However, the PCC must be reformulated before it can apply to Chinese. Consider a delegation context. In such a context, the simplex Chinese verb *anzhuang* 'install' in (3) maps onto a situation in the mental model that contains at least three events, namely the delegation event, the installing event and the becoming installed event. The PCC in (7) requires projection of the argument of the installing event and so cannot account for the Chinese delegation examples in (3). But a revision of the PCC along the lines in (9) would have the desired outcome:

(9) Revised PCC (RPCC): an external argument cannot be omitted if the event in which it is a participant overlaps with the verb's event of change.

The RPCC can explain why the compatibility with a delegation context is crucial for agent omission: when no delegation context is provided, the event in which the external argument participates is the installing event and that event overlaps with the becoming installed event. By contrast, in the delegation context, the external argument is an argument of a delegation event and that event does not overlap with the becoming installed event.

Although the RPCC is a step in the right direction, I will show that it is not empirically adequate. Since the RPCC states that whether agent omission is permitted is determined by the temporal relation between the event of change and the event in which the external argument is a participant, it predicts that the availability of agent omission will be completely determined by the mental model. So the pattern in (3) is expected to be also found in all the aspectual variants of the examples. However, when *anzhuang* is marked by the imperfective marker *-zhe* instead of *-zai*, agent omission is allowed even without a delegation context. In fact, agent omission in (10b) is even obligatory, which can be seen from (10a).

(10) a. #Zhangsan zai qiang shang anzhuang zhe kongtiao.
Zhangsan at wall on install ASP air-conditioner
Intended meaning: 'on the wall is installed an air-conditioner as a result of Zhangsan installing it.'

b. Kongtiao zai qiang shang anzhuang zhe.
air-conditioner at wall on install ASP
'On the wall is installed an air-conditioner.'

That different aspectual markers can lead to different results suggests that the correct formulation of the containment condition must be sensitive to aspect, and I argue that an aspect-based account is indeed viable. Indeed, I will defend the following hypothesis:

(11) The Aspectual Proper Containment Condition (APCC): An external argument is eliminated if and only if its referent does not participate in the eventuality denoted by the predicate in the interval yielded by aspect.

1 Introduction

Table 1.1 Definitions of the four aspectual markers

Aspectual markers	Definitions	Variations of interpretations
-zai	TT in the first phase of T-SIT	N/A
-zhe	TT in a single phase of T-SIT	Eventive: TT in the first phase of T-SIT; Stative (available only with 2-phase verbs): TT in the last phase of T-SIT
-le	TT covers a bound of T-SIT	Eventive: TT covers the end point of the source phase; Stative (available only with 2-phase verbs): TT covers the presupposition of a previous change-of-state event, which exists everywhere evenly in the target phase
-guo	TT in a single phase of T-SIT, which a presupposition that the phase it is located in has terminated	Eventive: TT in the first phase of T-SIT; Stative (available only with 2-phase verbs): TT in the last phase of T-SIT

Unlike the RPCC, the APCC is sensitive to the temporal relation between the running time of the event in which the external argument participates in the mental model and the interval yielded by aspect. The mental model represents our understanding of events, and the relations between events, in the world. When we produce an utterance containing a verbal predicate, the mental model contains a sequence of events that tokenizes the event denoted by the event variable of the verbal predicate. In terms of the aspect, I have adopted Klein et al.'s (2000) aspectual system, which defines aspect as the temporal relation between the time of situation (T-SIT) and the topic time (TT). The structure of T-SIT is determined by the event structure of the verb, while the alignment between T-SIT and TT varies with different aspectual markers. I have not adopted Klein et al.'s (2000) definitions for the four Chinese aspectual markers (-zai, -zhe, -le and -guo) but defended four alternative definitions based on the patterns found with the markers. In this monograph, they are defined as follows (Table 1.1).

Table 1.2 Distribution of 1-phase verbs

		Event	State
kao 'bake' $e_D(X, D)$ $e_1(D, Y)$	-zai	EA/ø	n/a
	-zhe	EA/ø	
	-le	EA/ø	
	-guo	EA/ø	
kao 'grill'		Event	State
tan gangqin 'play piano'	-zai	EA	n/a
xue roudao 'study judo'	-zhe	EA	
ai 'love'	-le	EA	
qian zhai 'owe debt' $e_1(X, Y)$	-guo	EA	
kai men 'open door' MM3		Event	State
	-zai	EA	n/a
$e_1(X, Y)$ & $e_s(Y)$	-zhe	EA	
	-le	EA	
	-guo	EA	

EA = external argument must be realised; ø = external argument must be omitted; EA/ø = external argument can be either realized or omitted

The diagrams represent the mental models (MM). e_D = delegation event; e_1 = acting event; e_2 = become event; e_s = result state; the capital letters in the brackets that follow the eventualities are the arguments of them: X = external argument; Y = internal argument; D = delegate, italicized because it is not projected)

External argument omission displays a complex distribution in Chinese, and I argue that the APCC makes correct predictions across the board. Here are two tables showing the distribution of 1-phase verbs and 2-phases verbs combined with the four aspectual markers respectively (Tables 1.2 and 1.3).

The APCC attempts to provide a novel account for the omission of external arguments in Mandarin Chinese through relating the presence/absence of the external argument to its participation during the interval specified by aspect. It captures numerous cases in Chinese in a way that can be easily explained in plain language: an event participant has to 'stay' (i.e., be realized) if they are doing something at the moment that is being talked about, and they have to leave (i.e., be omitted) if they do not.

Table 1.3 Distribution of 2-phase verbs

		Event	State
anzhuang 'install' $e_D(X, D)$ e1 (D, Y) & e2(Y) $e_s(Y)$	-zai	EA/ø	n/a
	-zhe	EA/ø(%)	ø
	-le	EA/ø	ø
	-guo	EA/ø	ø
hua 'draw' *tan quzi* 'play concerto' *die* 'fold' e1 (X, Y) & e2(Y) $e_s(Y)$		Event	State
	-zai	EA	n/a
	-zhe	EA	ø
	-le	EA	ø
	-guo	EA	ø
kai men 'open door' MM1 e1 (X, Y) e2(Y) $e_s(Y)$		Event	State
	-zai	EA	n/a
	-zhe	EA	ø
	-le	EA	ø
	-guo	EA	ø
kai men 'open door' MM2 e1 (X, Y) e2 (Y) $e_s(Y)$		Event	State
	-zai	EA	n/a
	-zhe	EA	ø
	-le	EA/ø	ø
	-guo	EA	ø
fang bianpao 'play firecrackers' e1 (X, Y) e2 (Y) $e_s(Y)$		Event	State
	-zai	EA/ø	n/a
	-zhe	EA/ø	n/a
	-le	EA/ø	ø
	-guo	EA/ø	n/a (irreversible)

References

Alexiadou, A., E. Anagnostopoulou, and F. Schäfer. 2015. *External arguments in transitivity alternations*. Oxford: Oxford University Press.

Klein, W., P. Li, and H. Hendriks. 2000. Aspect and assertion in Mandarin Chinese. *Natural Language & Linguistic Theory* 18 (4): 723–770.

Levin, B., and M. Rappaport Hovav. 1995. *Unaccusativity: At the syntax-lexical semantics interface*. Cambridge: MIT Press.

Rappaport Hovav, M., and B. Levin. 2012. Lexicon uniformity and the causative alternation. In *The Theta system: Argument structure at the interface*, 150–176. Oxford: Oxford University Press.

Reinhart, T. 2002. The Theta System—An overview (concepts interface). *Theoretical Linguistics* 28 (3): 229–290. https://doi.org/10.1515/thli.28.3.229.

Zhang, Y. 2022. No loitering: On the omission of external arguments in Mandarin Chinese. Doctoral Dissertation, University College London.

Open Access This chapter is licensed under the terms of the Creative Commons Attribution-NonCommercial-NoDerivatives 4.0 International License (http://creativecommons.org/licenses/by-nc-nd/4.0/), which permits any noncommercial use, sharing, distribution and reproduction in any medium or format, as long as you give appropriate credit to the original author(s) and the source, provide a link to the Creative Commons license and indicate if you modified the licensed material. You do not have permission under this license to share adapted material derived from this chapter or parts of it.

The images or other third party material in this chapter are included in the chapter's Creative Commons license, unless indicated otherwise in a credit line to the material. If material is not included in the chapter's Creative Commons license and your intended use is not permitted by statutory regulation or exceeds the permitted use, you will need to obtain permission directly from the copyright holder.

Chapter 2
Agent Omission with -*zai*

Abstract As the first chapter of the body-part, this chapter starts from the "unexpected" agent omission case in Chinese and considers it as a result of expletivization based on various tests. Agent omission, then, challenges the cross-linguistic generalization of UEAC, and the author proposes the M parameter to account for the Chinese agent omission without denying the validity of the UEAC. After the agent omission is legitimated, the next question is when the agent omission is allowed and when it is disallowed. A link between the availability of delegation reading and agent omission is found, which leads to the proposal of the core hypothesis, the APCC. The APCC is then applied to the -*zai* marked cases successfully.

Keywords Expletivization · The Proper Containment Condition · Aspectual marker -*zai*

2.1 Introduction

The causative alternation has been intensively studied in the literature as a cross-linguistic phenomenon. The verbs that can participate in this alternation have both a transitive use and an intransitive use. (12) shows a pair of examples from English.

(12)   a. John broke the window.
       b. The window broke.

There are verbs that can enter into the causative alternation and there are verbs that cannot, and what the rules and restrictions are that determine this has been widely discussed. Levin and Rappaport Hovav (1995), Reinhart (2002) as well as Alexiadou et al. (2015) propose the generalization that in order for a verb to allow the causative alternation, it has to be unselective in its external argument, i.e., either agent, instrument or causer must be allowed as the external argument. This generalization is named the *Underspecified External Argument Condition* (UEAC) by Alexiadou et al. (2015). It suggests that a verb that selects a specific thematic role for its external argument, e.g., an agent or a causer, cannot have an unaccusative alternate, which is borne out by examples like (13).

(13) a. John installed the air-conditioner.
　　 b. *The air-conditioner installed.

Admittedly, the UEAC is an imperfect generalization. As pointed out by Alexiadou et al. (2015), among the verbs compatible with expletivization, there are cases that disallow causers as well as cases that only allow causers. Therefore, the condition of 'unselectiveness' is not always respected cross-linguistically. Nevertheless, its successful prediction of the infelicity of (13b) suggests a core property of the causative alternation claimed by Alexiadou et al. (2015), which is that a verb that exhibits the alternation should not require the participation of an agent. Therefore, although there are counterexamples to the UEAC, it is predicted that there is no counterexample that involves selection of an agent as its external argument. When expressed in a feature system of the kind proposed by Reinhart, this core property is that an external argument specified by the predicate as [+m] (i.e., an argument whose mental state is implicated in the event denoted by the predicate) can never be reduced. Since the core property is assumed to hold cross-linguistically, the counterpart of (13b) is expected to be bad in any language that has the causative alternation.

Potential counterexamples to the UEAC are found in Mandarin Chinese, however, which seems to allow agent omission with certain predicates, as exemplified in (14).

(14)　Kongtiao　　　zai　　anzhuang
　　　air-conditioner　ASP　install
　　　'The air-conditioner is being installed.'

I will show through diagnostic tests that (14) should be regarded as a Chinese counterpart of (13b), where the agent is eliminated thoroughly. Examples like (14) are only permissible in certain contexts. This raises the further question what contextual constraints must be satisfied for agent omission to be felicitous. This in turn will require that we answer two questions: (i) what parameter is responsible for the difference between Chinese and English (as well as several other Indo-European languages) as regards the possibility of agent omission, and (ii) what restrictions the agent omission cases in Chinese are subject to.

To answer the first question, we will need a parameter that determines that the UEAC applies to some languages but not to the others, so that it is possible to account for the Chinese counterparts without denying the UEAC as a universal generalisation. In particular, I hypothesise that there are languages in which agentive verbs (that is, verbs whose meaning implicates actions by an agent) select the feature [+m] for their external argument, while other languages do not do so. I will call this the M parameter. English belongs to the first camp: agentive verbs grammaticalize their agentive nature by selecting the [+m] feature on their external argument. The result of this encoding is that the UEAC uniformly blocks the elimination of such external arguments in English. For languages like Chinese, the M parameter is set negatively: verbs whose meaning implicates the actions of an agent do not encode that meaning

2.1 Introduction

component through selection. Hence, the UEAC does not block elimination of the external argument. Of course, we would expect to find other languages that behave like Chinese, and Hindi-Urdu seems to be one of them (see Bhatt and Embick 2017).

The negative setting for the M-parameter has the consequence that, unlike their English counterparts, Chinese transitive agentive verbs are generally compatible with a context in which the actions of a [+m] actor qualify as delegation. The availability of delegation readings provides a hint for answering the second question, because contexts of delegation are found to feed agent omission in *-zai* sentences. The key point of this observation seems to be that the delegation context makes it possible for the external argument to 'not do anything' during the occurrence of the change of state, which follows straightforwardly from the Proper Containment Contain (PCC) proposed by Rappaport Hovav and Levin (2012):

(15) The Proper Containment Condition: When a change of state is properly contained within a causing act, the argument representing that act must be expressed in the same clause as the verb describing the change of state. (Rappaport Hovav and Levin 2012, 173)

Rappaport Hovav and Levin (2012) suggest that this condition rules out examples such as (16b), since the change of state is properly contained in the clearing act of the waiter. Van de Koot (lecture notes, 2019) points out that with a context where the waiter presses a button triggering a device in the counter that clears everything (16b) is felicitous, which further supports the Proper Containment Condition. The PCC is an extra-grammatical condition that restricts the mapping between a simplex causative verb and the representation of the event it denotes in the mental model (the mental model represents one's understanding of reality; see Johnson-Laird 1983).

(16) a. The waiter cleared the counter
 b. *The counter cleared. (Rappaport Hovav and Levin 2012, 172)

Another context in which the actions of the agent do not overlap with an event of change is one in which the agent is not a direct participant in the predicated event, but a 'delegator', such as in the second reading of (17).

(17) Lisi zai anzhuang kongtiao
 Lisi ASP install air-conditioner
 (i) 'Lisi is installing the air-conditioner.'
 (ii) 'Lisi is having someone install the air-conditioner.'

On the delegation reading the mental model contains a causing act in which Lisi assigns the installing task to the person who is to install the air-conditioner. This act does not temporally overlap with the installing event. Indeed, I will argue that (14) and sentences like it are only acceptable in delegation contexts, thereby providing further support for the crosslinguistic validity of the PCC.

However, since the PCC/RPCC determines whether an agent can be omitted based on the temporal relations between the events in the mental model of the verb, it predicts that a VP will always display the same pattern in terms of agent omission regardless of aspect. However, this is not the case. For example, the aspectual variant in (18) does not allow agent omission optionally, like (17) does, but forces it.

(18) Kongtiao   zai   qiang   shang   anzhuang   zhe
      air-conditioner at   wall   on   install   ASP
      'On the wall is installed an air-conditioner.'

(19) *Zhangsan   zai   qiang   shang   anzhuang   zhe   kongtiao
      Zhangsan   at   wall   on   install   ASP   air-conditioner
      Intended: 'on the wall there is an air-conditioner installed by Zhangsan.'

The contrast between the aspectual variants suggests that whether an external argument can be eliminated or not must be sensitive to aspect, and the RPCC is thus inadequate. To deal with this, I propose that Aspectual Proper Containment Condition (APCC):

(20) The Aspectual Proper Containment Condition (APCC): An external argument is eliminated if and only if its referent does not participate in the eventuality denoted by the predicate in the interval yielded by aspect.

In this chapter, I will show that the APCC not only does not sacrifice any results that the PCC obtains in English, but also accounts for the Chinese data that the PCC/RPCC fails to capture.

So far there are two constraints on agent omission. The UEAC is the grammatical constraint on event semantics, and the APCC is the extra-grammatical constraint on the relation between a simplex causative verb and the representation of the event it denotes in the mental model. The alternations ruled out by the UEAC cannot be rescued by any contexts, while those ruled out by the APCC are negotiable and can be improved significantly by an appropriate context. As mentioned above, (16b), which is ruled out by the PCC/APCC, is fine in a context in which the waiter presses a button to activate a mechanism that clears the table without further intervention of the agent. Contrastively, (13b) is ruled out by the UEAC, and its acceptability is not improved in any sort of context (such as a worker pressing a button to install the air-conditioner, although such a context is not pragmatically impossible).

The remainder of this chapter is organized as follows: Sect. 2.2 applies diagnostic tests to the agent omission structure to support the idea that the agent omission is the result of expletivization; Sect. 2.3 proposes the M parameter and shows that it can capture the cross-linguistic variability in the applicability of the UEAC; Sect. 2.4 proposes the Aspectual Proper Containment Condition (APCC) on the basis of the Proper Containment Condition (PCC) of Rappaport Hovav and Levin (2012) as the restriction determining whether an external argument can be eliminated; Sect. 2.6 considers the remaining questions; Sect. 2.7 concludes the chapter.

2.2 Agent Omission Is Expletivization

The causative alternation, which has been found cross-linguistically, yields verbs that have both a transitive use and an intransitive use, as illustrated in (21).

(21) a. John broke the window.
b. The window broke.
(22) a. John cut the bread.
b. *The bread cut.

Not all verbs can alternate, as is exemplified in (22), which has led to extensive discussion in the literature on which verbs can enter the alternation and which cannot. Levin and Rappaport Hovav (1995), Reinhart (2002) and Alexiadou et al. (2015) argue that a verb can only alternate if it is 'unselective' in its external argument. That is, its external argument is free to be an agent, an instrument or a causer. Alexiadou et al. (2015) capture this generalization with their *Underspecified External Argument Condition*, defined directly below.

(23) *Underspecified External Argument Condition*
(UEAC).

Those transitive verbs that cannot form anticausatives restrict their subjects to agents or agents and instruments and disallow causers. (Alexiadou et al. 2015, 53).

As for what the direction of the causative alternation is, there are different views in the literature. In this work, I adopt Reinhart's (2002) proposal that the anticausative variant is derived from the causative variant through an arity operation labelled expletivization (also known as decausitivization in Reinhart and Siloni (2005)), which is defined as an operation that eliminates the external argument. As for the restrictions on expletivization, Reinhart (2002) follows Levin and Rappaport Hovav (1995) and re-states their generalization in featural terms: expletivization only eliminates an underspecified [+c] theta role (i.e., a causer); it cannot eliminate a [+c + m] role.

The UEAC predicts successfully that *break* allows expletivization while *cut* does not, since *break* is compatible with an agent, an instrument or a causer as its external argument, while *cut* disallows a causer.

(24) a. The baker/the knife cut the bread.
b. *The lightening cut the clothesline.
c. *The bread cut.
(25) a. The vandals / the rocks / the storm broke the window.
b. The window broke. (Alexiadou et al. 2015, 53)

Alexiadou et al. (2015) point out that the UEAC is a strong but imperfect generalization, since there are counterexamples found in various languages. Some verbs that disallow causers can enter the causative alternation. For example, as shown in (26), motion verb *roll* in English licenses agent but not causer as the external argument, and it has an unaccusative use.[1] Moreover, some verbs that only allow causers are compatible with the alternation, too. One example of this verb class is German *anschwemmen* 'to wash ashore' (Schäfer 2008), which is illustrated in (27).

(26) a. John/*the wind rolled the ball.
  b. The ball rolled. (Alexiadou et al. 2015, 43)

(27) a. Der Fluss/*Der Mann   schwemmte den   Ast   an.
        the river / the man   washed   the   branch   ashore
   b. Der   Ast   schwemmte an.
        the   branch   washed   ashore   (Schäfer 2008, 122)

However, notwithstanding the counterexamples, Alexiadou et al. (2015) argue that UEAC represents the core property of the causative alternation, namely that in order for a verb to have an unaccusative alternation, it should not specify anything about the causing event, such as agentivity or intentionality.

Since the core property of the causative alternation is expected to hold crosslinguistically, it predicts that a verb that denotes an event involving the actions of an agent never alternates in any language that allows the causative alternation. Nevertheless, unexpectedly, counter-examples are found in Mandarin Chinese, such as the counterpart of (22) in (28) and its aspectual variant in (29).

(28) a. John/*dao   qie   le   mianbao
        John/*knife   cut   ASP   bread
        'John/*the knife cut the bread.'
   b. mianbao   qie   le
        bread   cut   ASP
        'The bread is cut.'

(29) a. John/*dao   zai   qie   mianbao
        John/*knife   ASP   cut   bread
        'John/*the knife is cutting the bread.'
   b. Mianbao   zai   qie
        bread   ASP   cut
        Lit. 'The bread is cutting.'
        'The bread is being cut.'

(28) is the exact Chinese counterpart of (22), while (29) is an aspectual variant of it. In what follows, I will concentrate on analysing (29b) rather than (28b). This is

---

[1] It could be argued that this is not an exception at all, if *roll* and other motion verbs are unergative that exceptionally allow their theme to be mapped internally. The transitive counterpart would then be derived by causativization. For extensive discussion of the difference between expletivization and causativization, see Horvath and Siloni (2011).

2.2 Agent Omission Is Expletivization

because (28b) could possibly be analysed as an adjectival passive, and thus does not have to challenge the UEAC. However, such an account is ruled out for (29b), since – unlike verbal passives – adjectival passives are incompatible with progressive aspect (Bruening 2014). This contrast is illustrated with the pair of English examples in (30).

(30)   a.   Harry is being beaten (by his opponent). (verbal passive)
       b.   *Harry is being unbeaten. (adjective in verbal environment) (Bruening 2014, 366)

Nevertheless, even if (29b) cannot be attributed to an adjectival passive structure, it is still too early to suggest that this is a challenge to the UEAC, since one may question whether (29b) is the result of expletivization or involves some other operation, such as topicalization across a null subject or saturation (i.e., passivization).

The potential analysis in terms of topicalization is based on the observation that in an agent omission example like (31a), the subject *kongtiao* 'air-conditioner' has to be the topic. This is shown through the observation that (31a) can only be an answer to (31b) but not to (31c).

(31)   a.   Kongtiao   zai   anzhuang
              air-conditioner   ASP   install
              'The air-conditioner is being installed.'
       b.   Kongtiao   ne?
              air-conditioner   Q.mark
              'Where is the air-conditioner?'
       c.   Nabian   zai   fasheng   shenme   shi?
              there   ASP   happen   what   thing
              'What is happening there?'

The answer to (31b) requires *kongtiao* 'air-conditioner' to be a topic, while the answer to (31c) has no topic. Therefore, the observation that (31a) cannot be a response to (31c) seems to suggest that (31a) is a topicalized structure interpreted as 'the air-conditioner, *pro* is installing'. In other words, it involves pro drop and topicalization of the theme argument. However, I argue that the fact that (31a) cannot be an answer to (31c) is due to other restrictions in Mandarin Chinese, which I will discuss now.

I agree with the observation that (31a) cannot be an answer to (31c), but I believe that this is not because it is an agent omission structure, but because it has a bare noun as its subject. According to Cheng and Sybesma (2005), in Mandarin Chinese, although bare nouns are compatible with either definite or indefinite interpretations, only the definite interpretation is possible with a bare noun that occurs pre-verbally. Therefore, (32) is expected to be semantically equivalent to (31a):

(32) Natai   kongtiao   zai   anzhuang.
     That-CL   air-conditioner ASP   install
     'The air-conditioner is being installed.'

Unexpectedly, different from (31a), (32) is an appropriate answer to (31c), which suggests that they are not completely equivalent. I thus hypothesise that a preverbal bare noun has to be interpreted as a topic. This hypothesis fits well with Cheng and Sybesma's (2005) proposal: since topics have to be definite, it is expected that preverbal bare nouns cannot have an indefinite interpretation. This hypothesis correctly predicts that a bare preverbal noun cannot be a focus:

(33) a. Q: Shui   zai   guo   malu?
         Who   ASP   cross road
         'Who is crossing the road?'
     b. A: Nage   nüren zai   guo   malu
         That-CL   woman ASP   cross road
         'That woman is crossing the road.'
     c. #A: Nüren zai   guo   malu
         Woman   ASP   cross road
         'A woman is crossing the road.'

(33) shows the same contrast with (31), which suggests that the fact that (31a) cannot be a reply to (31c) is not related to it being an agent omission structures, but exists everywhere that a bare noun occurs pre-verbally. Hence, we may conclude that we are not forced to adopt a pro drop + topicalization account for agent omission structures, even if some apparent cases of agent omission could be analysed along those lines. I will show how the pro drop cases can be teased apart from the cases that I treat as resulting from expletivization, which are the focus of this monograph. In the later chapters, I will further show that although the pro drop cases truly exist and thus present a potential confound in the study of agent omission, they are in fact correctly predicted by my core hypothesis and thus confirm it rather than challenge it.

Could (29b) be the result of saturation? The operation of saturation forms passives, and whether this is the case for (29b) is hard to tell simply from the sentence form, since Chinese is an isolating language and hence lacks verbal morphology that could be informative in this respect. However, the two operations differ from one another significantly in that saturation will not completely eliminate the agent argument, while expletivization reduces the agent entirely (Reinhart and Siloni 2005). This can be shown through several diagnostic tests. In the following part, I will use these tests to show that (29b) should be analysed as resulting from expletivization.

First, (29b) disallows agent-oriented modifiers. As is pointed out by Härtl (2003) and Koontz-Garboden (2009), the ability to take agent-oriented modifiers can differentiate inchoatives from passives. (34) shows this distinction in German (as well

2.2 Agent Omission Is Expletivization

as in its English translation). (35) and (36) shows that (29b) and (31a) pattern with inchoatives in this respect.

(34) a. Die Schüssel wurde absichtlich/leichtsinnigerweise/gerne zerbrochen.
'The bowl was broken on purpose/carelessly/willingly.'
b. *Die Schüssel zerbrach absichtlich/leichtsinnigerweise/gerne.
'*The bowl broke on purpose/carelessly/willingly.' (Härtl 2003, 892)

(35) Mianbao   zai   (*guyide /   *xinbuzaiyande / *xinganqingyuande) qie.
     bread   ASP   on purpose   carelessly   willingly   cut
     Lit. 'The bread is cutting (*on purpose/*carelessly/*willingly).'

(36) Kongtiao   zai   (*guyide /   *xinbuzaiyande/   *xinganqingyuande)
     air-conditioner ASP   on purpose   carelessly   willingly
     anzhuang.
     install
     Lit. 'The air-conditioner is installing (*on purpose/*carelessly/*willingly).'

Second, as claimed in Roeper (1987), whether a verb can control into a purpose clause is a diagnostic test for an explicit or implicit agent. (37) shows the different behaviours of expletivization and saturation with regard to this test. Again, (29b) and (31a) do not permit a purpose clause and hence must lack an agent entirely.

(37)
    a. *The boat sank to collect the insurance.
    b. The boat was sunk to collect the insurance.

(38) (*Wei-*le*   zhunbei   zaocan,)   mianbao   zai   qie
     in order to   prepare   breakfast   bread   ASP   cut
     Lit. 'The bread is cutting (*in order to prepare for the breakfast).'

(39) (*Wei-*le*   ganjue   nuanhuo,)   kongtiao   zai   anzhuang
     in order to   feel   warm   air-conditioner   ASP   install
     Lit. 'The air-conditioner is installing (*in order to feel warm).'

Third, (29b) and (31a) cannot license instruments. Reinhart and Siloni (2005) suggest that a reliable test for detecting whether an agent is present semantically in a predicate is its ability to license an instrument. For example, the unaccusative form of French *casser* 'break' is incompatible with an instrumental PP, as shown here in (40).

(40) *La   branche   s'est   cassée   avec   une   hache.
     the   branch   SE is   broken   with   an   axe
                              (Reinhart and Siloni 2005, 418)

Similarly, (29b) and (31a) cannot license instruments, either.

(41) Mianbao   zai   (*yong   daozi)   qie.
     bread   ASP   with   knife   cut
     Lit. 'The bread is cutting (*with a knife).'

(42) Kongtiao   zai   (*yong   luosidao)   anzhuang.
     air-conditioner ASP   with   screwdriver   install
     Lit. 'The air-conditioner is installing (*with a screwdriver).'

The three diagnostics above suggest that the operation that forms (29b) and (31a) eliminates the agent and thus should not be saturation. These diagnostics also suggest that the pro drop + topicalization account should not be applied to the examples above.

This should be contrasted with cases where the agent does not appear present but agentivity tests are passed. For example:

(43) (Wei-*le*   zaodian chifan,) natiao   yu   zai   (xiaoxinyiyide)
     in order to   early   eat   this-CL   fish ASP   carefully
     (yong   fenglide daozi)   chili.
     with   sharp   knife   handle
     '(In order to have meals early,) that fish has been (carefully) handled (with a sharp knife).'

(43), as an apparently agentless sentence, passes all three agentivity diagnostics, which suggests that it has a covert agent. As a result, (43) cannot be the result of expletivization. Instead, it can be possibly derived through saturation or pro drop + topicalization. I believe the latter is the account, since the sentence contains a topic. To be more specific, similar to my discussion on topicalization above, (43) can be an answer to (44a) which requires 'that fish' to be the topic of the answer, but it cannot be an answer to (44b), which does not have a topic at all. This contrast suggests that the example should be analysed as involving pro drop + topicalization rather than saturation.

2.2 Agent Omission Is Expletivization

(44) a. Natiao yu ne?
that-CL fish Q.mark
'Where is that fish?'
b. Nabian zai fasheng shenme shi?
there ASP happen what thing
'What is happening there?'

It may not appear easy to tease apart these pro drop cases from the real expletivization cases that I will study in this monograph, but I argue that the pro drop cases meet some requirements that the expletivization cases do not. The pro drop + topicalization cases are expected to (i) pass the agentivity tests and (ii) fail to be an answer to a non-topic question such as 'what is happening there?', while the expletivization cases should behave in exactly the opposite way. In the discussions above, I have already shown that (32) (repeated below as (45)) cannot pass the agentivity tests and at the same time can be an answer to 'what's happening there'. As a result, although some agentless cases should receive a pro drop account, it does not challenge my argument that (45) should be treated as derived through a thorough elimination of the external argument, i.e., expletivization.

(45) Natai kongtiao zai anzhuang.
That-CL air-conditioner ASP install
'The air-conditioner is being installed.'

The key to differentiating the pro drop cases from the expletivization cases is whether they can be an answer to a non-topic question rather than whether they can pass the agentivity tests. If an agentless case fails to pass the agentivity tests, we can confirm that it is derived by expletivization rather than through pro drop + topicalization. However, if the example passes the agentivity tests, we can only conclude that the example CAN have a structure that is pro drop + topicalization, but it is not strong enough to rule out the possibility that a homophonous expletivization counterpart exists at the same time. The expletivization account can be ruled out for an agentless example only if the example cannot be an answer to a non-topic question. All the critical examples analysed in this monograph will be checked through this test to make sure that they have (at least) an expletivization structure. I will also come back to this issue later in the coming chapters and further show that the pro drop cases are not only not a challenge to my core hypothesis, but rather support it. Due to the limit of space, however, I will not show the above tests for every example.

I thus conclude that the operation that yields (29b) and (31a) is expletivization. This in turn presents a challenge to the UEAC. We turn to this issue in the next section.

2.3 Agent Omission and the M Parameter

I have just shown that different from English, Chinese seems to allow agent omission, which presents a challenge to the UEAC. As a result, why Chinese can license agent omission in the first place needs to be accounted for. In this section, I will propose a parameter that captures why agent omission is allowed in Mandarin but not in languages such as English.

In Sect. 2.2, I reviewed Reinhart's (2002) work on the causative-unaccusative alternation. She names the operation that eliminates the external argument expletivization. Following Levin and Rappaport Hovav (1995), she re-states the UEAC in featural terms: expletivization is realized through an elimination of an external [+c] argument (i.e., a causer), and it is subject to a further condition that no [+m] roles can be eliminated. In order to make progress with capturing the distinction between English and Chinese, we should therefore consider the question of what forces the external argument of some verbs to be specified as [+m]. This feature is a reflex of the verb containing a manner component or a result component that is associated with actions by a [+m] individual. In other words, the mental state of some individual is implicated in the occurrence of the eventuality. If this is correct, then we may consider selection for [+m] the obligatory grammaticalization (that is, a syntactic encoding) of a specific interpretive property of the predicate. This encoding interacts with the UEAC, so that expletivization of the [+m] argument is blocked.

The UEAC is a constraint on the grammatical level, and it is non-negotiable: if a sentence is ruled out by the UEAC, no contexts can change the ungrammaticality. But the UEAC is not the only constraint on expletivization in English. Recall that in Sect. 2.3, I hypothesised that both English and Chinese are subject to the contextual constraint, i.e., the Proper Containment Condition. Therefore, for an external argument to be expletivized, English has to respect both the grammatical constraint, namely the UEAC, and the contextual constraint, namely the Proper Containment Condition.

I have proposed that Chinese is similar to English in obeying the contextual constraint, so the cross-linguistic difference in agent omission has to be attributed to variation in the applicability of the grammatical constraint, otherwise the agent omission cases in Chinese will be left without an account.

I suggest that the Chinese agent omission examples can be accounted for if we hypothesise that different from English, it is not the case that all verbs in Chinese encode the agent entailments of the verbal predicate through a selectional property of the external argument. Of course, the relevant semantics will require a context that supports these agent entailments, but it will not impose the requirement that these entailments must be fulfilled by the external argument. This will allow a delegator to occur as the external argument of an agentive verb in Chinese, while in English this is option is blocked.

Based on this hypothesis, Chinese requires satisfaction of the contextual constraint but not of the grammatical constraint for expletivization to occur. The absence of the grammatical constraint enables the delegation reading, and the delegation reading

2.3 Agent Omission and the M Parameter

further matches a proper context that satisfies the contextual constraint. As a result, agent omission becomes widely permissible in Chinese.

Whether a verb links a [+m] requirement to its external argument can be modelled as a parameter, where English and Chinese make opposite choices. I will refer to this as the M parameter. The effects of the UEAC only obtain in languages that require such a link, and therefore Chinese agent omission cases do not present a challenge to this condition.

The M parameter is best understood as a particular implementation of Bhatt and Embick's (2017) proposal that encyclopedic agentivity and grammatical agentivity should be distinguished from one another. Their proposal is grounded in Chomsky's (1970) and Marantz's (1997) works suggesting that some roots encode agentivity while some do not. These two types of roots are represented by $\sqrt{\text{DESTROY}}$ and $\sqrt{\text{GROW}}$ respectively. Although both *destroy* and *grow* can select agents as their external arguments, the derived nominals show different behaviours:

(46) a. The Romans destroyed the city.
　　 b. The Roman's destruction of the city…
(47) a. John is growing the tomatoes.
　　 b. *John's growth of the tomatoes.

Chomsky (1970) argues that the root $\sqrt{\text{GROW}}$ is not agentive per se, but becomes agentive in causative syntax. Based on the assumption that derived nominals are formed from roots rather than from verb structures, it is expected that *growth* has no agentivity. Contrastively, since the root $\sqrt{\text{DESTROY}}$ encodes agentivity, this property is also manifested in non-verbal environments, so that it allows the transitive nominalization *destruction*. Marantz (1997) further proposes that it is functional structure rather than the verb itself that licenses the external argument, and $\sqrt{\text{GROW}}$ only receives an agentive interpretation when it combines with this functional structure, while $\sqrt{\text{DESTROY}}$ is agentive on its own. Therefore, $\sqrt{\text{GROW}}$ and $\sqrt{\text{DESTROY}}$ show a difference in their *encyclopedic semantics*. Marantz (1997) claims that the agentivity in the encyclopedic semantics of $\sqrt{\text{DESTROY}}$ leads to the ungrammaticality of the unaccusative use in English:

(48)　*The city destroyed.

However, this correlation between the encyclopedic semantics and the syntactic structure does not have to hold in all languages. As observed by Bhatt (2009) and Bhatt and Embick (2017), in Hindi-Urdu, verbs such as *kat* 'cut' allow expletivization. They show through several diagnostic tests that in (49a), no implicit agent is present.

(49) a. Peṛ   kaṭ   rahe   hẼ
          trees.M   cut   Prog.MPI   be.Prs.Pl
          Lit: 'trees are cutting.' (i.e., trees are being cut.)
     b.   Kampani   peṛ   kaaṭ   rahii   hai.
          company.f   tree   cut   Prog.f   be.Prs
          'The company is cutting trees.'
                              (Bhatt and Embick 2017, 106)

Similar to √DESTROY, √CUT is also regarded as encyclopedically agentive. Since in English √CUT is not found with an unaccusative use (*<i>The trees cut</i>), (49) reflects a contrast between Hindi-Urdu and English in mapping from encyclopedic semantics to syntactic configurations. Bhatt (2009) and Bhatt and Embick (2017) thus suggest that grammatical agentivity and encyclopedic agentivity are distinct from each other. Encyclopedic agentivity entails grammatical agentivity in English, but not in Hindi-Urdu.

I argue that Chinese belongs in the same camp as Hindi-Urdu as regards the mapping between encyclopedic and grammatical agentivity and implement Bhatt & Embick's suggestion through the M parameter: only in English does encyclopedic agentivity in a root have obligatory effects in grammar, namely selection for a [+m] external argument.

2.4 The Aspectual Proper Containment Condition

After accounting for why Chinese is not restricted by the UEAC and thus allows agent omission, the next question is what rules the Chinese agent omission cases are subject to. Although the M parameter enables agent omission in Chinese, it does not mean Chinese allows agent omission in a completely free manner. There are well-formed agent omission cases, such as (14), repeated as (50); and there are also examples that disallows agent omission, such as (51):

(50) Kongtiao   zai   anzhuang.
      air-conditioner   ASP   install
      'The air-conditioner is being installed.'

(51) *Xiangrikui   zai   hua.
      sun-flower   ASP   draw
      Literally: 'the sunflowers are drawing.'
      Intended: 'the sunflowers are being drawn.'

2.4 The Aspectual Proper Containment Condition

Therefore, we need a rule that permits examples like (50) and rules out those like (51), and a breakthrough point can be found through an association between agent omission and delegation in the *-zai* examples.

2.4.1 Agent Omission and Delegation

Agent omission with *zai*-marked verbs has been rarely discussed in the literature. Li & Thompson (1994, 239–240) and Li (2015, 271) mention this structure but do not investigate it in any detailed way. Li and Thompson (1994) suggest that the agent omission structure has a non-agentive reading. They claim that an example like (52) becomes acceptable only with the advent of washing machines, which shows that a possible non-agentive background provided by world knowledge can feed this structure.

(52) Yifu   zai   xi.
     clothes ASP   wash
     'The clothes are washing.'

Li (2015) develops this idea further and proposes that the agent omission structure is allowed when it is 'possible to talk about the event from the perspective of the participant being acted upon and to construe the patient/theme argument and the verb as forming an event on their own (2015, 271).' He gives examples from both English and Chinese, as in (53) and (54), and suggests that the progressive aspect stativizes the event, namely, making it 'a state of continuously performing the same action' (2015, 271).

(53) Beans are cooking.
(54) Douzi   zai   zhu.
     bean   ASP   cook
     'The beans are cooking.'

(Li 2015, 272)

It seems that Li and Thompson (1994) and Li (2015) both hold the view that the agent omission structure with the progressive describes an event that takes place automatically. I agree that this property is shared by some examples with this structure. However, it only covers a small class of verbs (mainly cooking verbs), and examples like (29b) remain unaccounted for because they are acceptable in a context in which the event does not take place automatically (example (29b) does not require that the bread is cut by a machine). The question thus is: for those predicates that do not denote an automatic event, what makes them (in)compatible with the agent omission structure and why? Moreover, another significant question is whether there is an account that can cover both the automatic event cases and the non-automatic event cases.

Not all verbs are compatible with the agent omission structure with -*zai*, and which classes of verbs are allowed in this structure will be key to our understanding of agent omission. Verbs such as *anzhuang* 'install' and *zhuangxiu* 'renovate' seem to be perfectly compatible with the agent omission structure, as illustrated in (55) and (56). These examples are regarded as natural sentences by native speakers when uttered out of the blue. Some other verbs, such as *mai* 'buy', appear to be infelicitous in the agent omission structure when uttered without any contexts, but become much more acceptable under a certain context (see (57) and (58)). There are also verbs that are completely incompatible with agent omission, as shown in (59) – (61). Different from *mai* 'buy', these verbs cannot undergo agent omission even if similar contexts are provided.

(55)   Kongtiao   zai   anzhuang.
       air-conditioner   ASP   install

(56)   Fangzi   zai   zhuangxiu.
       house   ASP   renovate

(57)   (Context: a customer is buying books)
       *Shu   zai   mai.
       book   ASP   buy

(58)   (Context: the library of my university is purchasing a book for which I requested a loan. When I ask whether it has arrived, the librarian says, 'please bear with us…*shu zai mai*.')
       Shu   zai   mai.
       book   ASP   buy

(59)   *Youxi   zai   wan.
       game   ASP   play

(60)   *Mianbao   zai   chi.
       bread   ASP   eat

(61)   *Zhangsan   zai   da.
       Zhangsan   ASP   hit

I believe that the difference between (57) and (58) is key in figuring out the rule behind the agent omission cases. What the context in (58) brings in reflects the key contextual requirement of the agent omission structure in -*zai* examples. Comparing (57) and (58), what the context in (58) introduces seems to be a 'delegation' flavour. In other words, in (57), the buyer has to perform the buying action, while in (58), the librarian is not the buyer. Instead, he/she is simply communicating that the library staff have placed the book on order.

Beside the agent omission structures above, a delegation-like interpretation is also found in transitives cross-linguistically. Goldberg (1995, 168) notices the presence of this interpretation in English and refers to it as a *conventionalized scenario*.

2.4 The Aspectual Proper Containment Condition

Following Shibatani (1973), she claims that indirect causation can be expressed in simple causatives, provided they are 'conventionally accomplished in a particular way'. For example, in (62), Goldberg claims that the simple causative sentence can have such an interpretation because having painters paint the house is a conventional way of house-painting.

(62) She painted her house. (when in fact the painters did the painting)
(Goldberg 1995, 169)

However, these English cases seem to be quite limited. For an example like (63), it is difficult to obtain such a delegation reading, even though having your air-conditioner installed by an engineer is a conventional way of air-conditioner installing.

(63) Lisi is installing the air-conditioner. (#when in fact the engineer does the installing)

The licensing of the delegation reading appears to be more flexible in Mandarin than in English. Thus, the Mandarin counterpart of (63) in (64) is ambiguous, and allows the reading that Lisi is not the one carrying out the installing action, but a delegator of the task.

(64) Lisi zai anzhuang kongtiao.
 Lisi ASP install air-conditioner
  i) 'Lisi is installing the air-conditioner
  ii) Lisi is having someone install the air-conditioner.'

As the following examples show, the delegation reading appears to be correlated with the agent omission structure:

(65) a. Kongtiao zai anzhuang.
  air-conditioner ASP install
  'The air-conditioner is being installed.'
 b. Lisi zai anzhuang kongtiao
  Lisi ASP install air-conditioner
   i) 'Lisi is installing the air-conditioner.'
   ii) 'Lisi is having someone install the air-conditioner.'
(66) a. Fangzi zai zhuangxiu
  house ASP renovate
  'The house is being renovated.'
 b. Zhangsan zai zhuangxiu fangzi
  Zhangsan ASP renovate house
   i) 'Zhangsan is renovating the house.'
   ii) 'Zhangsan is having someone renovate the house.'

(67) a. (Context: the library is purchasing a book that I want to borrow. When I ask whether it has arrived yet, the librarian says, 'please bear with us…*book zai buy* now.')

Shu   zai   mai.
book   ASP   buy
'The books are being bought.'

b. (Context: a customer is buying books)

*Shu   zai   mai.
book   ASP   buy
'The books are being bought.'

c. Zhangsan   zai   mai   shu.
Zhangsan   ASP   buy   book
  i) 'Zhangsan is buying books.'
  ii) 'Zhangsan is having someone buy the books.'

(68) a. *Youxi   zai   wan.
game   ASP   play
Intended meaning: 'the game is being played.'

b. Zhangsan   zai   wan   youxi.
Zhangsan   ASP   play   game
'Zhangsan is playing the game.'
Not: 'Zhangsan is having someone play the game.'

(69) a. *Mianbao   zai   chi.
bread   ASP   eat
Intended meaning: 'the bread is being eaten.'

b. Zhangsan   zai   chi   mianbao.
Zhangsan   ASP   eat   bread
'Zhangsan is eating bread.'
Not: 'Zhangsan is having someone eat bread.'

(70) a. *Zhangsan   zai   da.
Zhangsan   ASP   hit
Intended meaning: 'Zhangsan is being hit.'

b. Lisi   zai   da   Zhangsan.
Lisi   ASP   hit   Zhangsan
'Lisi is hitting Zhangsan.'
Not: 'Lisi is having someone hit Zhangsan.'

The above data suggest that the delegation reading and agent omission are closely related. I thus propose the following hypothesis:

2.4 The Aspectual Proper Containment Condition

Hypothesis I: for a verb in the progressive aspect to allow agent omission, the verb must allow delegation.

(In other words: That X zai V Y has a delegation reading is a necessary condition for X zai V Y → Y zai V.)

The hypothesis can be interpreted in different ways. It could be that a group of verbs have certain intrinsic properties that allow both agent omission and the delegation reading, but that the two phenomena are independent from each other. Alternatively, the delegation reading matches the context required for agent omission, and the delegation flavour persists after the elimination of the agent. I argue the latter is the case, since the contrast between (57) and (58) indicates that the delegation context is significant in determining the acceptability of an agent omission example. Moreover, even for the agent omission examples that are regarded as natural without contexts (e.g., (55) and (56)), native speakers still tend to assume a delegation reading (i.e., the air-conditioner is being installed by others/the house is being renovated by others) when hearing the sentence out of the blue. This leads me to propose the adjusted hypothesis below:

Hypothesis II: X zai V Y → Y zai V requires a delegation context.

Note that in a delegation reading, the direct event participant, namely the event participant carrying out the activity denoted by the predicate, does not have to be [+m]. When the direct event participant is [+m], it is a case like (64): a person assigned an installing task by another person. If the direct event participant is not [+m], we are dealing with the case of automatic events discussed in the previous literature. This hypothesis thus covers both the automatic events discussed by Li and Thompson (1994) and Li (2015), as well as cases such as (65a), which are not accounted for by their proposals.

The revised hypothesis above appears to have some affinity with the Proper Containment Condition (PCC) proposed by Rappaport Hovav and Levin (2012). The PCC is a constraint on the causative alternation at the contextual level. Rappaport Hovav and Levin (2012) apply this condition to English and claim that (72b) is ruled out by this condition: since the causing act carried out by the waiter is properly contained in the change of state of the counter from not clear to clear, the expression of the agent is obligatory.

(71) The Proper Containment Condition: When a change of state is properly contained within a causing act, the argument representing that act must be expressed in the same clause as the verb describing the change of state.
(Rappaport Hovav and Levin 2012, 173)

(72) a. The waiter cleared the counter.
b. *The counter cleared. (Rappaport Hovav and Levin 2012, 172)

The PCC is extra-grammatical: it should be regarded as a condition on the mapping between simplex causatives and the mental model rather than on what is encoded in the verb. Context cannot affect a verb's semantics, but it does determine the causal chain in the mental model. (72b) is represented as (73) in the mental model. In (73), e_1 represents the event the waiter wiping the counter, and e_2 is the change of state that the counter becomes clear. Since e_2 is properly contained in e_1, according to the PCC, the argument of e_1 cannot be eliminated.

(73)
      e1(X,Y)
      └─────┘
        e2(Y)
        └────┘

    clear (X,Y) (ordinary context)

But the formulation of the PCC in (71) cannot be directly applied to Chinese cases like (65a). Since the PCC was originally proposed to account for English data, it presupposes that simplex causatives always involve direct causation, which is often assumed to be the case in English (but see Neeleman and van de Koot 2012 for a dissenting view), but is certainly not necessarily the case in Chinese. In the delegation reading of (65b), the simplex causative verb *anzhuang* 'install' maps onto a situation in the mental model involving a causal chain with a minimum of three events: the delegation event, the event involving the engineer and the becoming installed event. To deal with the Chinese data, the PCC must be able to consider the delegation event as well, but 'the causing act' in its original formulation fails to cover it.

I argue that the core of the PCC is that an external argument must be expressed if and only if it is an event participant during the occurrence of the change of state:

(74)   Revised PCC (RPCC): an external argument cannot be omitted if the event in which it is a participant overlaps with the verb's event of change

With this reformulation, it is easy to see why the presence of delegation can feed agent omission: when a delegation event exists, it is possible for the external argument, which is the delegator, to complete participation before the change of state starts to take place. For example, (64) and (65) show a pattern where delegation is available and agent omission is optional. The RPCC can capture this pattern, since the participation of the delegator can either overlap or not overlap with the change of state.

The RPCC seems adequate for capturing the agent omission data marked by -*zai*. However, it runs into problems when we consider examples marked by other aspectual markers (which I will discuss in detail in the following three chapters). For example, if *anzhuang* 'install' is marked instead by -*zhe* that yields a result state reading, the external argument will be forced to be absent, as is shown in (75) and (76):

(75)   Kongtiao   zai   qiang   shang   anzhuang   zhe
         air-conditioner   at   wall   on   install   ASP
         'On the wall is installed an air-conditioner.'

2.4 The Aspectual Proper Containment Condition

(76) *Zhangsan   zai   qiang   shang   anzhuang   zhe   kongtiao
       Zhangsan   at   wall   on   install   ASP   air-conditioner
       Intended: 'on the wall there is an air-conditioner installed by Zhangsan.'

(75) and (76) show a pattern in which delegation is available while agent omission is obligatory, different from their -*zai* counterparts in (64) and (65). This is not accounted for by the RPCC, since they are considered the same in terms of the temporal relation between the participation of the delegator and the change of state. This suggests that the RPCC is still inadequate, and we need an updated version that is sensitive to aspect.

What makes the -*zhe* examples above different from their -*zai* counterparts is that although the participating time of the external argument optionally overlaps with the aspectual interval specified by -*zai*, it can never overlap with the aspectual interval specified by -*zhe*. To be more specific, since -*zai* yields a progressive reading, the aspectual interval should be located within the running time of the installing event; in the meantime, as -*zhe* marks a result state reading, the aspectual interval should be aligned with the installed state that the event culminates in. (77)–(79) show the temporal relation between a series of eventualities that tokenize the event denoted by the event variable of the verb (at the top) and the aspectual interval (at the bottom). As for the installing example, e_D represents the delegation event, e_1 the installing event, e_2 the become event and e_s the result state. The symbol '&' between e_1 and e_2 indicates that they occur simultaneously. The capital letters in the brackets show the participants of the eventualities, with X representing the delegator, which is the external argument; D representing the delegate, who is the actual 'doer' of the installing event (italicized because it is not projected in the argument structure); and Y representing the theme, namely the air-conditioner. In this mental model, e_D is always the event in which the external argument X participates. (77) and (78) illustrate the possible situations for the -*zai* examples: the aspectual interval can either overlap with e_D or not. Contrastively, (79) shows the situation for the -*zhe* examples, where the aspectual interval aligns with the result state and can never overlap with e_D. This contrast matches the patterns above, since agent omission is optional in the -*zai* examples but obligatory in the -*zhe* examples.

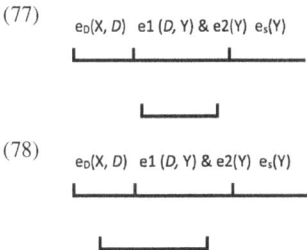

(77) $e_D(X, D)$ e1 (*D*, Y) & e2(Y) e_s(Y)

(78) $e_D(X, D)$ e1 (*D*, Y) & e2(Y) e_s(Y)

(79)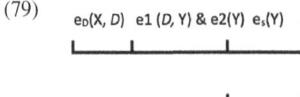

I thus propose an updated version of the PCC that links the presence/absence of the external argument with aspect. I dub this the Aspectual Proper Containment Condition (APCC):

(80) The Aspectual Proper Containment Condition (APCC): An external argument is eliminated if and only if its referent does not participate in the eventuality denoted by the predicate in the interval yielded by aspect.

This hypothesis involves the temporal relation between the cluster of eventualities that tokenize the event denoted by the event variable of the verb and the interval specified by the aspect. The former is referred to as the mental model, which represents one's understanding of the reality. The latter is named as 'the topic time' (TT) in Klein et al.'s (2000) aspectual system, which is the system I will adopt in this study. In the following parts, I will give detailed explanations of these concepts.

2.4.2 The Three Tiers of the APCC

The APCC involves alignment between events in the mental model and the interval denoted by aspect. According to Klein et al.'s (2000) proposal, aspect is defined as the relation between the time of situation (T-SIT) – the running time of the event denoted by the verb – and the topic time (TT). Therefore, the APCC concerns the alignment between three tiers, namely the mental model, T-SIT and TT. In the following part I will introduce both the mental model and T-SIT/TT based on Klein et al.'s (2000) theory to prepare for the data analysis with the APCC.

The mental model of verbs is 'constructed on the basis of their meaning and any relevant general knowledge of the world' (Johnson-Laird et al. 1992, 420). It represents one's perception of the reality in the discourse, and the information it conveys is more complex than the verbal expression it is constructed on (Johnson-Laird 1983). For example, although *anzhuang* 'install' is compatible with delegation, it does not mean its event structure contains a delegation event e_D. Instead, the complicated cluster of eventualities form the mental model, including the delegation event where Zhangsan assigned the installing task to a person, the causing event where the person installed the air-conditioner, the become event that the air-conditioner becomes installed gradually, which takes place simultaneously with the causing event, and a result state of the air-conditioner being installed.

The time of situation (abbreviated T-SIT), in Klein et al.'s (2000) aspectual system, refers to the running time of the situation denoted by the verbal expression. The

2.5 Accounting for the Data with the APCC

number of phases that T-SIT contains varies across different verb types. Individual-level states, such as a number being odd or even, are treated as 0-phase verbs as they do not have a beginning and an end. Stage-level states or activities, which are atelic predicates, are considered as 1-phase verbs. Their T-SIT starts from the moment that the situation obtains and is followed by the time it does not obtain anymore. The telic predicates, including accomplishments and achievements, are seen as 2-phase verbs, which contain a change of state within the time span. The T-SIT of 2-phase verbs consists of a source phase and a target phase, separated by the moment that the state changes. *Anzhuang* 'install' is telic and thus is a 2-phase verb. Its source phase covers the time when the air-conditioner was under installation and its target phase is the time of the result state that the air-conditioner has been installed. Therefore, the target phase of T-SIT always aligns with e_s in the mental model, and with the delegation context, e_D, e_1 and e_2 all fall in the source phase.

T-SIT is determined by the verbal expression per se and thus is independent from aspect. What different aspects determine is the third tier we need to discuss, which is the topic time (TT). Klein et al. (2000) defines TT as 'the time span about which something is said' (742). The situation denoted by the verb is fixed, but the speaker can view this situation from different stages: they can make an assertion of the ongoing event, which is an imperfective aspect, or they can describe an event that has occurred and then completed, which is a perfective aspect, and this difference is reflected in the alignment between TT and T-SIT. Different aspects thus should be defined as the different relations between TT and T-SIT. Klein et al. (2000) suggest that these relations can be represented in terms of how TT overlaps with T-SIT and the post-time/pre-time of T-SIT. In this monograph, I will adopt TT as the aspectual interval in the APCC. Since T-SIT can align with both the mental model and TT, it is possible to see the temporal relation between the mental model and TT, which is the core point for determining the presence/absence of an external argument in the APCC. In 2.5, I will apply the APCC to examples with different verb types to show how these three tiers work.

2.5 Accounting for the Data with the APCC

Before capturing the *-zai* data with the APCC, we need to first make clear how *-zai* should be defined in the Kleinian system. This definition seems to be quite straightforward: *-zai* is an imperfective marker that is similar to the English progressive, which is defined as TT in the first phase of T-SIT.[2] In the case of a 1-phase verb, TT

---

[2] The original formation of Klein et al.'s definition for *-zai* concerns a notion named the Distinguished Phase (DP) that varies cross-linguistically. For a 1-phase verb, DP is the only phase of the verb; for a 2-phase verb, DP is the first phase (source phase) in English and the second phase (target phase) in Chinese, and Klein et al. (2000, 754) define *-zai* as 'TT in T-DP'. I do not follow Klein et al. (2000) in using the term 'DP' as the progressive/stative ambiguity found with *-zhe* suggests that the concept of DP is not as necessary as it is supposed to be, which I will discuss in the next chapter.

locates within the only phase of T-SIT; in the case of a 2-phase verb, TT is contained properly in the source phase of T-SIT.

(81) -zai   TT in the first phase of T-SIT

In the following analyses, I will investigate examples with different verb types, present diagrams with the three tiers discussed above and show how the APCC makes the correct predictions regarding omission of the external argument.

2.5.1 1-Phase Verbs

Since we have seen that whether delegation is available leads to different types of mental models, it is important to categorize the examples with regard to whether they are compatible with delegation. 1-phase verbs include activities and states, and it should be noted that the progressive marker -*zai* is incompatible with states. This is not unexpected, since the English progressive does not combine with states either.

(82)   *Zhangsan   zai   ai   qizi.
       Zhangsan   ASP   love   wife
       Literally: 'Zhangsan is loving his wife.'
(83)   *Zhangsan is loving his wife.

Therefore, in the following analysis, I will only consider activities marked by -*zai*. 'Baking a cake' is an activity that allows delegation, since the baking process is done by the oven automatically. As a result, the mental model will contain a delegation event e_D, followed by a baking event e_1. T-SIT only has one phase, namely the source phase, which aligns with the sum of e_D and e_1. Since -*zai* is defined as TT in the first phase of TT, it locates within the only phase of T-SIT in this case, and there are thus two possibilities with its alignment with the mental model:

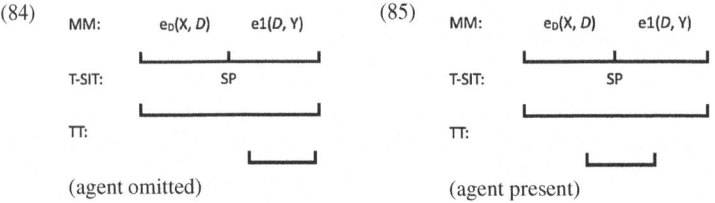

With TT staying within T-SIT, it can either avoid overlapping with e_D (illustrated in (84)) or overlap with it (illustrated in (85)). In the case of (84), the external argument X does not participate during TT, so the APCC predicts that the external argument should be omitted. Contrastively, in (85), since X's participation overlaps with TT, the APCC predicts that the external argument has to be projected. Therefore, when

2.5 Accounting for the Data with the APCC

this verbal expression is marked by -*zai*, the prediction from the APCC is that the external argument can either be present or absent, and this is borne out, as shown in (86) and (87):

(86) Dangao   zai   kao
     cake   ASP   bake
     'A cake is being baked.'

(87) Zhangsan   zai   kao   dangao
     Zhangsan   ASP   bake   cake
     'Zhangsan is baking a cake.'

As for the activities that do not permit delegation, we can take one example from the list in Sect. 2.4.1:

(88) *Zhangsan   zai   da
     Zhangsan   ASP   hit
     Intended: 'Zhangsan is being hit.'

(89) Lisi   zai   da   Zhangsan
     Lisi   ASP   hit   Zhangsan
     'Lisi is hitting Zhangsan.'
     Not: 'Lisi is having someone hit Zhangsan.'

(89) is incompatible with a delegation context as it cannot be interpreted as 'Lisi is having someone hit Zhangsan'. Therefore, its mental model will not contain a delegation event, but a hitting event e_1 only, which aligns with the only phase of T-SIT. TT, as -*zai* is defined, is positioned in T-SIT and thus is also in e_1.

(90)   MM: $e_1(X,Y)$
           T-SIT: SP
           TT:

As the diagram shows, the external argument X inevitably participate in the event during TT, so the APCC predicts that the external argument can by no means be omitted, and the ungrammaticality of (88) supports this prediction.

2.5.2 2-Phase Verbs

The 2-phase verbs should also be categorized into two types based on whether they permit delegation. The two example I have given at the beginning of 2.4 and their agentive counterparts can represent the two types respectively. The examples are repeated as follows:

(91) Kongtiao   zai   anzhuang.
     air-conditioner   ASP   install
     'The air-conditioner is being installed.'

(92) Zhangsan   zai   anzhuang   kongtiao.
     Zhangsan   ASP   install   air-conditioner
     'Zhangsan is installing the air-conditioner.'
     Or: 'Zhangsan is having the air-conditioner installed.'

(93) *Xiangrikui   zai   hua.
     sun-flower   ASP   draw
     Literally: 'the sunflowers are drawing.'
     Intended: 'the sunflowers are being drawn.'

(94) Zhangsan   zai   hua   xiangrikui.
     Zhangsan   ASP   draw   sun-flower
     'Zhangsan is drawing sunflowers.'
     Not: 'Zhangsan is having the sunflowers drawn.'

In the case of (91) and (92), the mental model consists of a delegation event e_D, an installing event e_1, a become event e_2 that takes place at the same time with e_1, and a result state e_s at the end. T-SIT contains a source phase that aligns with e_D, e_1 and e_2, and a target phase that aligns with e_s. Since -*zai* locates TT in the first phase of T-SIT, TT will be contained in the source phase of T-SIT. Therefore, similar to the case of activities with delegation that we have discussed above, there are two possible alignments between TT and the mental model, As is shown in (95) and (96):

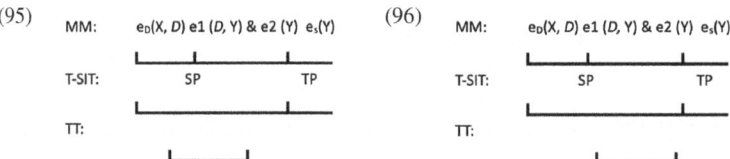

In (95), the delegation event e_D, which is the event in which the external argument X participates, overlaps with TT. Therefore, the APCC predicts that the external argument should not be eliminated. In (96), contrastively, TT does not overlap with e_D, so the prediction from the APCC will be that the external argument must be omitted. These two possibilities suggest that the omission of the external argument in (92) is optional, which is confirmed by the data.

2.5 Accounting for the Data with the APCC　　　　　　　　　　　　　　　37

(93) and (94) present situations incompatible with delegation. Their corresponding mental model thus lacks the delegation event e_D. Only the simultaneous e_1 and e_2 are left, followed by the result state e_s. The source phase of T-SIT aligns with e_1 and e_2, while the target phase aligns with e_s. TT, as required by -*zai*, is covered by the source phase of T-SIT. In this case, TT and the mental model have to be aligned as in (97).

(97)
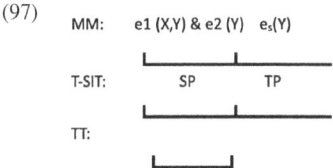

In (97), the external argument X has to be an event participant during TT. The APCC thus predicts that the external argument must be present, which is borne out in (93) and (94).

2.5.3 Examples with Inalienable Possessors

I hypothesised in Sect. 2.4 that the presence of the delegation reading of *X zai V* is a necessary condition for *X zai V Y* → *Y zai V*, but I did not say it is also a sufficient condition. This is because of an exception found with inalienable possessors, as exemplified in (98).

(98)　a.　　*Ya　　zai　　ba.
　　　　　　tooth　ASP　　extract
　　　　　　Intended: 'The tooth is being extracted.'
　　　b.　　John　zai　　ba　　ya.
　　　　　　John　ASP　　extract　tooth
　　　　　　i) 'John is extracting a tooth.'
　　　　　　ii) 'John is having his tooth extracted.'

As is shown in the translations, (98b) also has the delegation reading, i.e., John does not have to be the one who extracted the tooth; he can also be the possessor of the tooth. In these cases, the event in which the external argument participates (i.e., the delegating acts) do not have to overlap with TT, which seems to match the alignments in (96), and the agent is thus expected by the APCC to be omitted. However, this delegation reading does not feed agent omission as it does in other cases above, since (98a) is infelicitous.

What differentiates (98b) from examples such as (92) seems to be that the external argument in (98b) is an inalienable possessor of the referent of the internal argument. In other words, the referent of the internal argument is a component (*pars*) of the referent of the external argument (*toto*). John possesses his teeth in an inalienable way, and that means whenever the teeth are involved in an event in the mental model, it is entailed that John participates in that event. To be more specific, in contrast to the air-conditioner installation case, where the delegator can be doing anything when the engineer installs the air-conditioner, if John's wisdom teeth are being extracted, it is impossible for John to be absent. Therefore, the mental model in (96) is not the correct illustration for (98b): X should participate in e_1 and the become event e_2, too, together with the internal argument Y. Therefore, (98) should be analysed as (99):

(99)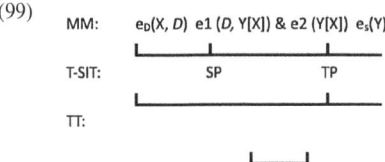

Given (99), the APCC precisely accounts for (98a) and (98b): the agent X, as the inalienable possessor of Y, inevitably participates in e_1, and hence it has to participate during the interval of TT. Agent omission is therefore blocked.

2.5.4 Another Look at the English Data

In the following discussion, I will return to the English examples accounted for by the PCC in Sect. 2.4.1 to investigate whether they can also be covered by the APCC. (72a)/ (72b) and their aspectual variants are repeated as follows.

(100) a. *The counter cleared. (Rappaport Hovav and Levin 2012, 172)
  b. The waiter cleared the counter.
(101) a. *The counter is clearing.
  b. The waiter is clearing the counter.

Note that the expletivization of the verb *clear* is not ruled out by the UEAC because the verb does not select [+m] external arguments particularly. A cause can also be its external argument, as is shown in (102). After it is allowed by the UEAC, the APCC is at play at the extra-grammatical level.

(102) The wind cleared the counter.

Since the English verb *clear* is incompatible with a delegation context, the diagram in (97) can be used to show alignment of TT in the source phase. Since the agent

2.5 Accounting for the Data with the APCC

X inevitably participates in the clearing event during TT, the agentless progressive variant (101a) is ruled out by the APCC.

Like the PCC, the APCC can also account for the English perfective case in (100). According to the definition given by Klein et al. (2000), perfective aspect in English has TT overlapping with SP and the post-time of SP, as shown in (103). Again, the agent X cannot avoid participating in the interval of TT and thus cannot be omitted.

(103)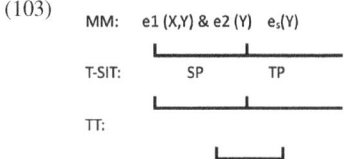

The acceptability of the agentless variants can be improved given proper contexts, however. As pointed out by Hans van de Koot (lecture notes, 2019), it is possible to leave 'the waiter' unprojected in a context where the waiter simply presses a button to clear the counter automatically.

(104)   a. The waiter cleared the counter (by pressing a button).

         b. The counter cleared.

(105)   a. The waiter is clearing the counter (by pressing a button).

         b. The counter is clearing.

I argue that this intriguing contrast can also be captured by the APCC. This button-pressing context corresponds to a different mental model, which contains a button pressing event e_1 and a become event e_2, with e_1 taking place before e_2 (which is in a sense close to the delegation). Thus, (104a) and (105a) have the representations in (106) and (107), respectively, where X participates in the event during TT and hence has to be projected.

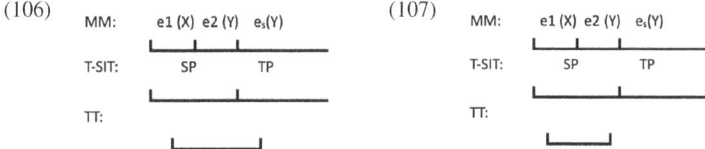

Nevertheless, TT in (106) and (107) can also be shorter and thus does not overlap with e_1, as shown in (108) and (109). As a result, the APCC will forces agent omission, and this is exactly the case of (104b) and (105b).

(108) 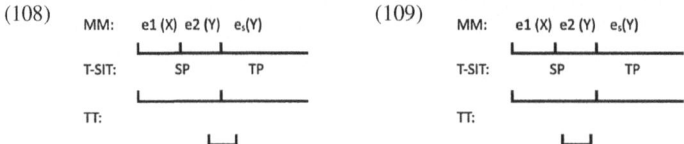 (109)

(108) and (109) may not be the only possible representations for (104b) and (105b), though, as the two examples can also be regarded as pure unaccusatives, which are associated with a mental model that lacks the button-pressing event (the counter becomes clear automatically), and yield the alignment patterns in (110) and (111). Since the mental model has no causer participant, this argument is also not projected in the syntax.

(110) 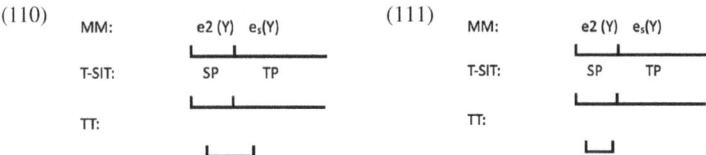 (111)

Both the mental models can capture the absence of the agent in (104b) and (105b), and it seems that the only way to check which one is preferred is using temporal modifiers. We can suppose that the waiter has to turn on the machine by logging onto a computer, opening an app and pressing the button, which in total take one minute; after that, the clearing of the counter takes another minute. That is to say, e_1 and e_2 each last for 1 min, so the running time of SP in (108)/(109) is 2 min while that in (110)/(111) is 1 min. Under this context, it seems that native speakers accept (112a) but not (112b). This suggests that speakers may tend to always minimise the mental representation of unaccusative events.

(112)   a. The counter cleared in 1 min.
        b. The counter cleared in 2 min.

Comparing (97)/(103) and (110)/(111), we can see that the key difference provided by the new context that enables the agent omission is that the become event unfolds all by itself. With such a become event, the agent avoids participating in TT, so its absence is well captured by the APCC.

2.6 Remaining Questions

Although my hypothesis accounts for why the agent omission cases are allowed in Chinese so far, there is still something unsolved. Firstly, we have seen that whether a verb marked by -*zai* is compatible with delegation is related to whether its external

2.6 Remaining Questions

argument can be omitted, but what determines whether it is compatible with delegation or not? Secondly, it remains unclear whether agent omission verbs should be categorized as unaccusative. However, as I show below, they differ from unaccusatives in several respects.

2.6.1 When Is Delegation Available?

Although Mandarin seems to be more lenient in licensing the delegation reading than English, it still has restrictions, as shown through the existence of infelicitous examples. As I have shown, the mental model is the representation of the reality in the discourse. It is not a representation stored with lexical items in the lexicon. Nevertheless, the observation that not all verbs allow delegation suggests that the compatibility with delegation should be information that is stored in the lexicon. If so, any there any rules for the compatibility?

I was inspired by Cançado (2010) and Cançado and Gonçalves' (2016) analysis of a phenomenon in Brazilian Portuguese referred to as the agent-beneficiary alternation. Sentences that have this alternation have a reading that resembles the delegation reading discussed above.[3]

(113) a. O rapaz lavou o carro de Maria.
the boy washed the car of Maria
'The boy washed Maria's car.'

b. Maria lavou o carro (com o rapaz).
Maria washed the car (with the boy)
'Maria had her car washed (by the boy).'

c. O empregado lavou o carro da Maria (com o rapaz).
the employee washed the car of Maria (with the boy)
'The employee had Maria's car washed (by the boy).' (Cançado 2010, 5).

Levin and Rappaport Hovav (1995), following Smith (1970), define two verb types, namely internally caused verbs and externally caused verbs. For an internally caused verb, its external argument has some inherent property that is responsible for bringing about the eventuality the verb denotes (e.g., *play*, *eat* and *sing*); contrastively, for an externally caused verb, there is an external cause that brings about the eventuality (e.g., *wash*, *write* and *break*). Cançado and Gonçalves (2016) suggest that being an externally caused verb is a necessary condition for the agent-beneficiary alternation.

---

[3] Although the agent-beneficiary alternation found in Brazilian Portuguese appears to be semantically close to the delegation reading, it cannot be captured by my account for the delegation reading, and I make no attempt to fully account for the alternation in this chapter. I hold the view that the phenomena found cross-linguistically that are close to the delegation reading can be yielded through different processes, and what process the agent-beneficiary alternation results from requires further investigation.

A restriction to external causation could also explain why some verbs disallow the delegation reading in Mandarin, e.g., the 'play' and 'eat' in examples (68) and (69). That no internally caused verbs allow delegation, if correct, is logically understandable. If the inherent property of the external argument is selected by the verb, it is no surprise that the external argument cannot be replaced with a different NP that is a delegator, since the inherent property does not belong to the delegator.

However, this restriction is still insufficient, since there exist transitive verbs that are not categorized as internally caused but that still do not allow the agent omission. For example, the verb *da* 'hit':

(114) a. *Lisi zai da.
       Lisi zai hit
       Intended meaning: 'Lisi is being hit.'
    b. Zhangsan zai da Lisi.
       Zhangsan zai hit Lisi
       'Zhangsan is hitting Lisi.'

Da 'hit' is categorized as an externally caused verb based on Levin and Rappaport Hovav's (1995) definition, so the absence of a delegation reading in (114b) is still unaccounted for. Nevertheless, it appears that this Mandarin verb semantically entails that the external argument has physical contact with the internal argument. A contrast can be seen in the following examples:

2.6 Remaining Questions

(115) Zhangsan zai da   Lisi, *dan ta   wanquan meiyou pengdao Lisi.
      Zhangsan zai hit Lisi   but   he   at all   not   touch   Lisi
      'Zhangsan is hitting Lisi, #but he is not touching Lisi at all.'

(116) Zhangsan zai anzhuang kongtiao,
      Zhangsan zai install   air-conditioner
      dan ta wanquan meiyou pengdao kongtiao.
      but he at all   not   touch   air-conditioner
      i) 'Zhangsan is installing the air-conditioner, but he is not touching the air-conditioner at all.'
      ii) 'Zhangsan is having someone install the air-conditioner, but he is not touching the air-conditioner at all.'

The physical contact of the external argument also seems to be an inherent property of it, and in this sense *da* 'hit' is closer to the internally caused verbs such as *chi* 'eat'. I have also tested some other activities that require no physical contact of the external argument, and they all seem to be compatible with the delegation reading and the agent omission. Some examples are shown as follows.

(117) a. Wenjian   zai   xiazai.
         file   zai   download
         'The file is downloading.'
     b. Zhangsan   zai   xiazai   wenjian.
         Zhangsan   zai   download   file
         'Zhangsan is downloading the file.'
(118) a. Zoulang   zai   xiaodu.
         corridor   zai   sterilize
         'The corridor is being sterilized.'
     b. Zhangsan   zai   xiaodu   zoulang.
         Zhangsan   zai   sterilize   corridor
         'Zhangsan is sterilizing the corridor.'

Admittedly, the restriction of physical contact captures the case of 'eat' in (69), since one has to have physical contact with the food when eating it, but I argue that this does not make the restriction on the internally caused verbs unnecessary. This is because of (68), repeated here as (119).

(119) *Youxi   zai   wan.
       game   ASP   play
       Intended meaning: 'the
       game is being played.'

(119) can be captured by the internally caused verb restriction, since *wan* 'play' is an internally caused verb; in the meantime, it cannot be accounted for by the physical contact restriction, since playing something does not necessarily involve physical contact. One example is to play some virtual games, which are not touchable. I therefore argue that both the internally caused verb restriction and the physical contact restriction are necessary to account for the cases that disallow the delegation reading. Since these verbs lack the delegation reading, they have no available contexts that meet the APCC, and thus are incompatible with agent omission.

2.6.2 Are Agent Omission Verbs Unaccusatives?

The sections above have not yet covered the question how the agent omission verbs should be categorized. It appears that these verbs show some unaccusative properties, but in other respects behave differently from canonical unaccusatives.

As I have shown in Sect. 2.2, the agent omission structure lacks agentivity entirely. It has been suggested by numerous scholars that in the unergative/unaccusative dichotomy of intransitive verbs, unergatives project agents while unaccusatives lack such an argument (Perlmutter 1978; Pinker 1989; Pustejovsky 1995; Levin and Rappaport Hovav 1995; Sorace 2000 among others). Based on this dichotomy, it would seem that agent omission verbs should be treated as unaccusative verbs. Bhatt and Emick (2017) also regard the *kat* 'cut' case in Hindi-Urdu (see example (49a)) as unaccusative, presumably based on the absence of agentivity.

However, a problem for suggesting the agent omission verbs as unaccusatives is that these verbs do not behave like typical Mandarin unaccusatives. According to Huang (1990), Mandarin unaccusatives have the property that the theme can occur either pre-verbally or post-verbally. For example:

(120) a. Sange   ren   si   le.
         three-CL   person   die   ASP
      b. Si   le   sange   ren.
         die   ASP   three-CL person
         'Three people died.'

However, in the agent omission structure, the theme cannot appear in the object position:

(121) *Zai   anzhuang   kongtiao
       ASP   install   air-conditioner
       Intended meaning: 'the air-conditioner is being installed.'

Based on these considerations, it is difficult to determine whether the agent omission verbs should be regarded as unaccusative verbs or not. On the one hand, since I treat these verbs as resulting from expletivization, unaccusatives seem to be the only possible category for them. On the other hand, if they are treated as unaccusatives, the question why they behave differently from canonical unaccusatives in various respects will need an answer.

Nevertheless, it should be admitted that there are still numerous unaccusative puzzles so far. Scholars have pointed out that *Unaccusative Mismatches* are found in various languages (Zaenen 1993; Levin and Rappaport Hovav 1995; Alexiadou et al. 2004). *Unaccusative Mismatches* refers to the situations where a verb is positive for some unaccusative tests but negative for others. For example, for the unergative/unaccusative dichotomy in Dutch, prenominal perfect participle, auxiliary selection and impersonal passivization are three significant diagnostic tests (see Levin and Rappaport Hovav 1995; Perlmutter 1978; Zaenen 1993 among others). A Dutch unaccusative verb is expected to be able to occur as a prenominal perfect participle, select BE rather than HAVE and reject impersonal passivization. However, some verbs are found with mixed behaviours, such as *blijven* 'stay' and *bloeden* 'bleed':

(122) a. De   *gebleven/   *gebloede   jongen
         the   stayed   bled   boy
     b. De   jongen   is   gebleven/   gebloed.
         the   boy   is   stayed   bled
     c. Er   wordt   *gebleven/ *gebloed.
         there   was   stayed   bled
                              (Alexiadou et al. 2004, 9)

As is shown in (122), *bloeden* 'bleed' behaves like an unergative verb in the prenominal perfect participle test, but like an unaccusative verb in the other two tests. Based on these mismatched situations, the indeterminacy found with the agent omission verbs seems to be less surprising than one might expect. This is an interesting topic that calls for further exploration, and it may bring up some insights into verb typology in Mandarin Chinese.

2.7 Conclusion

This chapter has discussed the agent omission cases marked by *-zai*, which I have analysed as expletivization. Expletivization is normally assumed to be restricted to arguments that are not [+m] as expressed by the UEAC, so why can it apply to Chinese agents? I conjectured that while the UEAC is inviolable, English and Chinese differ in whether the agentive entailments of the root are grammatical codified as selection for [+m]. I called this the M parameter and proposed that Chinese (like various other languages) is negatively specified for this parameter. Thus, while in languages such as English an agentive verb selects a [+m] external argument, in languages like Mandarin the [+m] requirement is not a part of the verbal semantics. As a result, although expletivization in Mandarin is still subject to other restrictions, it is more lenient and yields cases that are not allowed in English. The M parameter hypothesis leads one to expect that there are more historically distinct languages that make the same choice as Mandarin Chinese in terms of the M parameter. Hindi-Urdu seems to be one of them.

The M parameter explains why agents can be omitted in Chinese in the first place, but the restrictions that the agent omission phenomenon in Chinese is subject to are still not fully clear. Based on the Proper Containment Condition (Rappaport Hovav and Levin 2012), I have proposed the Aspectual Proper Containment Condition (APCC) to associate the presence/absence of the external argument to the aspectual interval. More in particular, the APCC states that an agent is eliminated if and only if it does not participate in the event denoted by the predicate in the time interval specified by aspect. The APCC accounts for the cases with -*zai* and the English cases successfully.

References

Alexiadou, A., E. Anagnostopoulou, and M. Everaert. 2004. *The unaccusativity puzzle: Explorations of the Syntax-Lexicon interface*. Oxford: Oxford University Press.

Alexiadou, A., E. Anagnostopoulou, and F. Schäfer. 2015. *External arguments in transitivity alternations*. Oxford: Oxford University Press.

Bhatt, R. 2009. Structural properties of implicit arguments. Paper presented at the University of Massachusetts at Amherst, Semantics Seminar.

Bhatt, J., and D. Embick. 2017. Causative derivations in Hindi-Urdu. *Indian Linguistics* 78 (1–2): 93–151.

Bruening, B. 2014. Word formation is syntactic: Adjectival passives in English. *Natural Language & Linguistic Theory* 32 (2): 363–422.

Cançado, M. 2010. Verbal alternations in Brazilian Portuguese: A lexical semantic approach. *Studies in Hispanic & Lusophone Linguistics* 3(1).

Cançado, M., and A. Gonçalves. 2016. Lexical semantics: Verb classes and alternations. *The Handbook of Portuguese Linguistics* 374: 391.

Cheng, L.L.S., and R. Sybesma. 2005. Classifiers in four varieties of Chinese. *Handbook of Comparative Syntax* 259–292.

Chomsky, N. 1970. Remarks on nominalization. In *Readings in English transformational Grammar*, ed. R.A. Jacobs and P.S. Rosenbaum, 184–221. Boston: Ginn Blaisdell.

Goldberg, A.E. 1995. *Constructions: A construction grammar approach to argument structure*. Chicago: University of Chicago Press.

Härtl, H. 2003. Conceptual and grammatical characteristics of argument alternations: The case of decausative verbs. *Linguistics* 41 (5): 883–916.

Horvath, J., & T. Siloni. 2011. Causatives across components. *Natural Language and Linguistic Theory* 29: 657–704.

Huang, C.T.J. 1990. Two kinds of transitive and intransitive verbs in Chinese. In *Proceedings of the Second Meeting of the World Chinese language association*, ed. Peng-cheng Dong, 39–59. Taipei: World Chinese Language Association.

Johnson-Laird, P.N. 1983. *Mental models: Towards a cognitive science of language, inference, and consciousness*. Cambridge: Harvard University Press.

Johnson-Laird, P.N., R.M. Byrne, and W. Schaeken. 1992. Propositional reasoning by model. *Psychological Review* 99 (3): 418–439.

Klein, W., P. Li, and H. Hendriks. 2000. Aspect and assertion in Mandarin Chinese. *Natural Language & Linguistic Theory* 18 (4): 723–770.

Koontz-Garboden, A. 2009. Anticausativization. *Natural Language & Linguistic Theory* 27 (1): 77.

Levin, B., and M. Rappaport Hovav. 1995. *Unaccusativity: At the syntax-lexical semantics interface*. Cambridge: MIT Press.

Li, C. 2015. Event structure and argument realization. *SKY Journal of Linguistics*, 28.

Li, C.N., and S.A. Thompson. 1994. On 'middle voice' verbs in Mandarin. *Voice: Form and Function* 27, 231.

Marantz, A. 1997. No escape from syntax: Don't try morphological analysis in the privacy of your own lexicon. *University of Pennsylvania working papers in linguistics* 42, 14.

Neeleman, A., & H. van de Koot. 2012. The linguistic expression of causation. *The Theta System: Argument structure at the interface*, 37.

Perlmutter, D. 1978. Impersonal passives and the Unaccusative Hypothesis. In *Proceedings of the Fourth Annual Meeting of the Berkeley Linguistics Society*, 157–189.
Pinker, S. 1989. *Learnability and cognition: The acquisition of argument structure*. Cambridge: MIT Press, MA.
Pustejovsky, J. 1995. *The generative lexicon*. Cambridge: MIT Press.
Rappaport Hovav, M., and B. Levin. 2012. Lexicon uniformity and the causative alternation. In *The Theta system: Argument structure at the interface*, 150–176. Oxford: Oxford University Press.
Reinhart, T. 2002. The Theta System—An overview (concepts interface). *Theoretical Linguistics* 28 (3): 229–290. https://doi.org/10.1515/thli.28.3.229.
Reinhart, T., and T. Siloni. 2005. The lexicon-syntax parameter: Reflexivization and other arity operations. *Linguistic Inquiry* 36 (3): 389–436.
Roeper, T. 1987. Implicit arguments and the head-complement relation. *Linguistic Inquiry* 18 (2): 267–310.
Schäfer, F. 2008. The syntax of (anti-)causatives. *External arguments in change-of-state contexts*. Amsterdam: John Benjamins.
Shibatani, M. 1973. A linguistic study of causative constructions. Doctoral Dissertation. University of California, Berkeley.
Smith, C. 1970. Jespersen's move and change class and causative verbs in English. *Linguistics and literary studies in honor of Archibald A. Hill* 2, 101–109.
Sorace, A. 2000. Gradients in auxiliary selection with intransitive verbs. *Language* 76 (4): 859–890.
Zaenen, A. 1993. Unaccusativity in Dutch: Integrating syntax and lexical semantics. In *Semantics and the lexicon*, ed. J. Pustejovsky, 129–161. Dordrecht.

Open Access This chapter is licensed under the terms of the Creative Commons Attribution-NonCommercial-NoDerivatives 4.0 International License (http://creativecommons.org/licenses/by-nc-nd/4.0/), which permits any noncommercial use, sharing, distribution and reproduction in any medium or format, as long as you give appropriate credit to the original author(s) and the source, provide a link to the Creative Commons license and indicate if you modified the licensed material. You do not have permission under this license to share adapted material derived from this chapter or parts of it.

The images or other third party material in this chapter are included in the chapter's Creative Commons license, unless indicated otherwise in a credit line to the material. If material is not included in the chapter's Creative Commons license and your intended use is not permitted by statutory regulation or exceeds the permitted use, you will need to obtain permission directly from the copyright holder.

Chapter 3
Agent Omission with *-zhe*

Abstract In this chapter, the APCC is applied to the agent omission cases marked by *-zhe*, which is found in both the locative inversion structure and the canonically ordered structure. Since the contrast between the *-zai* cases and the *-zhe* cases is the exact motivation for the proposal of the APCC, this chapter gives a discussion on how the APCC has been developed in a more detailed manner, and at the same time successfully captured all the *zhe* marked cases with the APCC.

Keywords APCC · Locative inversion · Aspectual marker *-zhe*

3.1 Introduction

In this chapter, I will apply the APCC to account for the agent omission phenomenon with the aspectual marker *-zhe* in Chinese. *-zhe* is found in both the locative inversion structure and the canonically ordered structure and I will cover both in this chapter. The two structures are illustrated in (123) and (124), respectively.

(123) Qiang   shang   anzhuang   zhe   kongtiao.
       wall   on   install   ASP   air-conditioner
       'On the wall is installed an air-conditioner.'

(124) Kongtiao   zai   qiang   shang   anzhuang   zhe.
       air-conditioner at   wall   on   install   ASP
       'On the wall is installed an air-conditioner.'

(123) and (124) provide examples of agent omission with the aspectual marker *-zhe*. The verb *anzhuang* 'install' is an accomplishment that selects an agent as its external argument. This agent, however, is not realised in (123) and (124). I will show in a later section—through the application of several agentivity diagnostics—that the agent is completely eliminated rather than covertly present. In fact, agent omission in (123) and (124) is not just allowed, but forced, which is shown in (125) and (126):

(125) #ᵃQiang   shang   Zhangsan   anzhuang   zhe   kongtiao.
       wall   on   Zhangsan   install   ASP   air-conditioner
       Intended meaning: 'on the wall is installed an air-conditioner as a result of Zhangsan installing it.'

(126) #Zhangsan   zai   qiang   shang   anzhuang   zhe   kongtiao.
       Zhangsan   at   wall   on   install   ASP   air-conditioner
       Intended meaning: 'on the wall is installed an air-conditioner as a result of Zhangsan installing it.'

ᵃ(125) and (126), as well as (134b) below, are unacceptable as the agentive counterparts of (123)/(124)/(133b), which have a stative reading. However, they are acceptable or at least marginally acceptable when interpreted as progressive, which I will investigate in Sect. 3.4.2

This suggests that (123) and (124) have a pattern that is different from their aspectual variant (127), where the agent can be either omitted or projected.

(127) Kongtiao   zai   anzhuang
      air-conditioner   ASP   install
      'The air-conditioner is being installed.'

In the previous chapter, I observed that a necessary condition for agent omission in a -*zai* sentence is a delegation context. That is to say, the reason why (127) is felicitous is because (128) has a reading on which Zhangsan is having another person install the air-conditioner for him. Contrastively, although a delegation context is compatible with (123) and (124), it is unfortunately not required. Even if the person uttering (123) and (124) was the installer, which is a context where no delegator exists at all, (123) and (124) still sound natural. In contrast, if the speaker of (127) is installing the air-conditioner on their own, (127) becomes inappropriate. In short, the delegation context is a prerequisite for agent omission with -*zai* in (127), but not for agent omission with -*zhe*, as in (123) and (124).

(128) Zhangsan   zai   anzhuang   kongtiao.
      Zhangsan   ASP   install   air-conditioner
      i) 'Zhangsan is installing the air-conditioner.'
      ii): 'Zhangsan is having the air-conditioner installed.'

There are thus two differences between the -*zhe* and -*zai* variants above. Firstly, the -*zai* examples optionally allow agent omission, while the -*zhe* counterparts obligatorily require it; secondly, for an agent to be eliminated, the presence of a delegation context is necessary for the -*zai* examples but not for the -*zhe* examples. The contrast found between the -*zhe* and -*zai* variants above motivates the proposal of the APCC. As I have discussed in Chapter 2, a reformulation of the PCC (RPCC) is enough to account for the pattern of (127)/(128), but not for (123)/(125) and (124)/(126).

3.1 Introduction

(129)   Revised PCC (RPCC): an external argument cannot be omitted if the event in which it is a participant overlaps with the verb's event of change.

The RPCC makes the relation between agent omission and the delegation context found in *-zai* examples understandable. This is because with the delegation context, the delegating event in the mental model is the event that the external argument participates in, and the nature of the delegation context determines that the change of state event does not overlap with the delegating event. Thus, the RPCC predicts that agent omission is possible where the delegation context is compatible in *-zai* examples.

However, the condition runs into problems when we turn to (123) and (124). Since the RPCC attributes whether an external argument can be omitted or not to the tokenization of the event denoted by the VP only, that the aspectual variants of (127)/(128) display a different pattern is unexpected. Since in a non-delegation context, the event that the external argument participates in (i.e., the installing event) inevitably overlaps with the event of change (i.e., the event of the air-conditioner becoming installed), the current formulation of the PCC incorrectly predicts (123) and (124) to be bad.

I have already proposed the APCC as the alternative solution to account for the external argument omission cases marked by *-zai* in Chapter 2, which claims that the presence/absence of the external argument should be sensitive to aspect. However, since it is the difference between the *-zai* examples and *-zhe* examples that has motivated the APCC from the very beginning, I will give a detailed discussion on how the APCC is proposed and developed in this chapter.

(130)   The Aspectual Proper Containment Condition (APCC): An external argument has to be eliminated if and only if it does not participate in the eventuality denoted by the predicate in the interval yielded by aspect.

I have shown in Chapter 2 that the APCC not only does not sacrifice any of the results previously obtained from the PCC, but also makes correct predictions for all the cases of agent omission with *-zai*. In this chapter, I will further account for the agent omission phenomenon with the aspectual marker *-zhe*, with the APCC to show that it makes correct predictions across the board.

The chapter is organised as follows. Section 3.2 introduces the different readings that *-zhe* can yield as well as the different types of Chinese locative inversion structures. It also discusses the distinction between the existential construction (ExC) and the locative construction (LoC) and restricts the scope of this chapter to LoC with *-zhe*. Section 3.3 investigates the different cases of agent omission with *-zhe* in both canonically ordered sentences and in LoC, and accounts for them with the APCC. Section 3.4 revisits the cases discussed in the previous chapter, and shows that the APCC captures them correctly. Section 3.5 concludes the chapter.

3.2 Basic Facts About LoC and *-zhe*

Since this chapter deals with the aspectual marker *-zhe* in both canonically ordered sentences and in locative inversion structures, in this section, I will first introduce the locative inversion structure in Chinese, and then go through the various readings that can be obtained when *-zhe* combines with different types of VPs.

3.2.1 Types of the Locative Inversion Structure

The locative inversion structure is a typical pattern with non-canonical word order that has been found cross-linguistically. In this structure, a locative phrase occupies the pre-verbal position, while the subject is located post-verbally. (131a) and (131b) present an English and a Mandarin Chinese locative construction, respectively.

(131) a. On the wall hangs a picture.
       b. Qiang   shang   gua   zhe/le   yifu   hua.
           wall   on   hang   ASP   1-CL   picture
           'On the wall hangs a picture.'

One significant topic of study in the area of locative inversion are the thematic restrictions on the structure. For English, it has been debated whether unaccusatives are the only verbs that appear in the locative inversion structure (see Bresnan and Kanerva 1989; Bresnan 1994), or whether unergatives are allowed in this structure as well (Levin and Rappaport Hovav 1995). There have also been suggestions that unergatives are only possible when the post-verbal Determiner Phrase is heavy (so-called heavy inversion; Culicover and Levine 2001; Paul et al. 2019). I will not look into this debate since it is beyond the scope of this chapter, but an important conclusion that can be drawn from it is that agentive transitives are never allowed in English locative inversion (Cornish 2005).

By contrast, in Mandarin Chinese, unaccusatives, unergatives and transitives are all permitted in the locative inversion construction. However, before further discussion of the compatible verb categories in Chinese locative inversion, we need to tease apart two structures that both appear to have a locative inversion pattern. Paul et al. (2019) suggest that under the pattern of PlaceP V DP, there are in fact two different constructions in Mandarin Chinese, namely the existential construction (ExC) and the locative construction (LoC). They point out that ExC does not require the PlaceP and is only compatible with unaccusatives, while LoC requires the PlaceP and allows unaccusatives, unergatives as well as transitives. LoC is represented in (131b), and ExC is illustrated in (132).

3.2 Basic Facts About LoC and -zhe

(132)   (Jia   li)   lai   le   keren.
           home   in   come   ASP   guests
           'There have come guests at home.'

Paul et al. (2019) argue that the choice of verbs in ExC is limited. Among unaccusatives, only verbs denoting (dis)appearance (e.g., *lai* 'come', *dao* 'arrive', *si* 'die', etc.), the existential verb *you* 'have' and weather verbs are allowed in ExC. These verbs do not involve agents inherently. Moreover, as shown in several empirical studies (Liu 2007; Shan and Yuan 2007; Laws and Yuan 2010), this type of unaccusative is incompatible with *-zhe*. Since what I will discuss in this chapter is agent omission with *-zhe*, ExC has no relevance to the topic. In what follows, I will focus on LoC.

As mentioned earlier, LoC in Chinese permits unaccusatives, unergatives and transitives. (131b) is an example with an unaccusative verb, while (133a) and (133b) illustrate LoC with an unergative and a transitive verb, respectively.

(133)   a.   Beimen   shang   shou   zhe/le[a]   yige   lian.
               North.Gate   on   guard   ASP   1-CL   company
               'At the North Gate a company keeps guard.' (Paul et al. 2019, 30)
      b.   Qiang   shang   anzhuang   zhe/le   kongtiao.
               wall   on   install   ASP   air-conditioner
               'On the wall is installed an air-conditioner.'

[a] Paul et al. (2019) only give the example with the aspectual marker *-zhe*. That it is also compatible with *-le* is my judgement.

The verbs in (133a) and (133b) are agentive, with the agent realised in (133a) but absent in (133b). Both examples are relevant to our enquiry: (133a) does not permit agent omission (its agent is obligatorily present; see (134a)), whereas (133b) appears to be the result of agent omission. With this stative reading, its agent can be realised when the aspectual marker is *-le* rather than *-zhe*, which is shown in (134b). In the following sections, I will argue that examples like (133b) indeed involve agent omission, and that (133a/133b) and (134a/134b) can all be accounted for by one single hypothesis.

(134) a. *Beimen   shang   shou   zhe/le.
       North.Gate on   guard   ASP
       Intended meaning: 'At the North Gate someone keeps guard.'
    b. Qiang   shang Zhangsan anzhuang le/   kongtiao.
                                          #¹zhe
       wall   on   Zhangsan install   ASP   air-conditioner
       'On the wall there is an air-conditioner installed by Zhangsan.'

(134b) shows a contrast between *-le* and *-zhe* in (dis)allowing agents in LoC, and there are different views on this contrast in the literature. Hu (1995) and Djamouri and Paul (2017) observe that the state denoted by *-le* LoC sentences must be the result of prior human actions while that is not the case for the state denoted by *-zhe* LoC sentences. They point out that in a context where there is no such prior action, only *-zhe* is compatible, as shown in (135).

(135) Shushao   shang gua   *le/zhe yilun   ming   yue.
      tree.top on   hang   ASP   one-CL   bright   moon
      'The bright moon is hanging over the top of the tree.' (Hu 1995, 106)

Djamouri and Paul (2017) thus propose that in *-zhe* LoC, no agent role exists, either overtly or covertly. Paul et al. (2019) follow this suggestion and further claim that different from *-zhe* LoC, *-le* LoC has an implicit agent. These views directly follow Pan's (1996) proposal that the agent is syntactically dropped in *-le* LoC but completely deleted in *-zhe* LoC, which is why the agent can be lexicalised in *-le* LoC but not in *-zhe* LoC. This agent deletion, Pan suggests, is triggered by *-zhe*. Not all *-zhe* marked agentless sentences have undergone agent deletion, though, as Pan claims that the agent deletion operation only applies to verbs with an argument structure < agent, theme, location > , but not to verbs with only < theme, location > . Therefore, in (135), *gua* 'hang' should be treated as a pure stative verb rather than a transitive verb according to Pan (1996).

I will investigate *-zhe* LoC in this chapter and *-le* LoC in the next chapter. I agree with Pan (1996) that the agents in the *-zhe* marked sentences are deleted thoroughly, but I will propose a different account for why and when the agents are deleted and argue that it is a better solution that generalizes successfully to all the current cases of LoC.

3.2.2 The Definition of -zhe

-zhe LoC is an important structure for studying the behaviour of *-zhe*, but it is not the only structure in which *-zhe* appears. As I have shown in the beginning of this chapter,

---

[1] As I have suggested in Footnote.4, *-zhe* receives a hashtag rather than a star here because it is incompatible in a stative reading but accepted by some native speakers in the progressive reading.

3.2 Basic Facts About LoC and -zhe

-*zhe* can also occur in canonically ordered sentences. In the following part, I will investigate how -*zhe* behaves in the two structures when combining with different types of verbs and propose a definition for this aspectual marker.

The aspectual marker -*zhe* has been regarded as an imperfective or durative marker in the literature. Smith (1997) and Yeh (1993) treat -*zhe* as marking result states. This definition matches the semantics of (123) and (124), repeated as (136) and (137) for convenience:

(136) Qiang   shang   anzhuang   zhe   kongtiao.
      wall   on   install   ASP   air-conditioner
      'On the wall is installed an air-conditioner.'

(137) Kongtiao   zai   qiang   shang   anzhuang   zhe.
      air-conditioner at   wall   on   install   ASP
      'On the wall is installed an air-conditioner.'

However, the resultative stative use does not seem to be the only use of -*zhe*. -*zhe* is found with either a progressive reading or a stative reading depending on the verb it attaches to, which has been widely noticed in the literature. Lü (1980, 523) proposes that -*zhe* marks the continuation of an activity or the duration of a state. Li and Thompson (1989, 236) define -*zhe* as marking 'an ongoing posture or state resulting from an activity'. Dai (1997) points out that -*zhe* shows the progressive/stative duality, and which reading -*zhe* receives is influenced by the verb type and whether the agent is present or not. Admittedly, the progressive reading of -*zhe* is less frequently used and natural than its stative use, and it seems to be subject to some pragmatic and dialectical factors. Klein et al. (2000) suggest that compared to the pure progressive marker -*zai*, -*zhe* is more common in written texts than in spoken language. Smith (1997) points out that in some northern dialects of Chinese, -*zhe* can be used to replace -*zai*. That said, (138), as a -*zhe* sentence with a progressive reading, is still acceptable to native speakers and it becomes completely natural when related to a second clause with the complementizer *yibian…yibian* ('while', literally 'one side…one side'), as shown in (139).

(138) Zhangsan   anzhuang   zhe   kongtiao.
      Zhangsan   install   ASP   air-conditioner
      'Zhangsan is installing an air-conditioner.'

(139) Zhangsan   yibian   anzhuang   zhe   kongtiao,
      Zhangsan   one-side   install   ASP   air-conditioner
      yibian   he   women   shuohua.
      one-side   with   we   talk
      'Zhangsan is installing an air-conditioner while talking to us.'

Comparing (137) and (138), we can see that -*zhe* shows the progressive/stative ambiguity when combining with an accomplishment such as *anzhuang* 'install'. The accomplishment, a 2-phase verb, as suggested by Klein et al. (2000), makes the ambiguity possible. Unsurprisingly, when -*zhe* combines with an activity, which is 1-phase, only the progressive reading is possible.

(140) Zhangsan kao   zhe   dangao.
       Zhangsan bake ASP   cake
       'Zhangsan is baking a cake.'

(141) Kaoxiang li   kao   zhe   dangao.
       oven   in   bake ASP   cake
       'A cake is being baked in the oven.'

Now the question is how -*zhe* should be defined. In dealing with aspect, I follow Klein et al. (2000), who introduce an aspectual system that defines aspect as the alignment between the time of situation (T-SIT) and topic time (TT). Klein et al. (2000) define -*zhe* as (142):

(142) -*zhe*   TT in the only phase of 1-phase verbs and the second phase of 2-phase verbs[2]

This definition predicts that -*zhe* will yield a result state reading when combining with an accomplishment and a progressive reading with an activity. Both these predictions are borne out, as previously illustrated in (136), (137), (140) and (141). However, the progressive reading of the accomplishment *anzhuang* 'install' shown in (138) and (139) is not accounted for. Therefore, (142) cannot be entirely correct.

The two readings with the accomplishment and the single reading with the activity suggest that TT can locate within any phase, but never overlaps with two phases at the same time. Therefore, I suggest that -*zhe* should be defined as (143):

(143) -*zhe*   TT in a single phase of T-SIT

This matches Smith's (1997, 276) proposal that -*zhe* 'presents a moment or interval of a situation S that includes neither endpoint, and does not precede I/E (the initial point of an event)'. -*Zhe* should therefore be defined as an imperfective marker, which aligns TT within one phase. When it combines with a 1-phase verb, TT locates within the only phase; when it combines with a 2-phase verb, TT can locate within either the first phase, named the source phase (SP), or the second phase, named the target phase (TP). These temporal relations between T-SIT and TT are illustrated in the following diagrams.

---

[2] Klein et al.'s original definition for -*zhe* is 'TT in T-DP'. As I have suggested in Footnot.2, I do not use the notion 'DP' as the progressive/stative ambiguity found with -*zhe* suggests that the concept of DP is not as necessary as it is supposed to be.

3.2 Basic Facts About LoC and -zhe   57

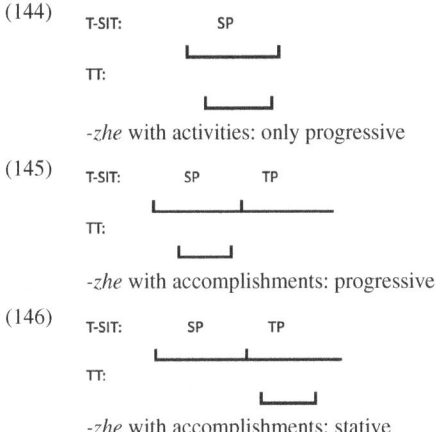

(144) T-SIT: SP
      TT:
      -zhe with activities: only progressive

(145) T-SIT: SP   TP
      TT:
      -zhe with accomplishments: progressive

(146) T-SIT: SP   TP
      TT:
      -zhe with accomplishments: stative

Based on this definition of -zhe, I will proceed to investigate the relation between agent omission and aspect in the next section and propose an aspectual condition that can capture the various cases of agent omission with -zhe.

3.2.3 No Implicit Agent with -zhe

I have shown in the beginning of this chapter that although *anzhuang* 'install' is an agentive verb, its agent can remain unprojected. However, before treating the relevant examples as cases of agent omission, agentivity tests should be applied to make sure the missing agents are completely eliminated rather than covertly present.

(147)   Kongtiao   zai   qiang   shang   anzhuang   zhe.
        air-conditioner at   wall   on   install   ASP
   i) 'On the wall is installed an air-conditioner.'
   ii) 'An air-conditioner is being installed on the wall.'

A canonically ordered agentless sentence like (147)[3] can be tested via several agentivity diagnostics, such as agent-oriented modifiers, instrument licensing and purpose clauses, as shown in (148a/b/c). The example fails to pass these tests in both the stative reading and the progressive reading.

---

[3] As Footnote 4 has covered, the progressive reading needs a proper context to sound more natural. In the following part, I will present the progressive reading without commenting on this point again, until Sect. 3.4.2 where I will come back to discuss this reading.

(148) a. Kongtiao   (*xinbuzaiyande/   *xinganqingyuande)
          air-conditioner   carelessly   willingly
          zai   qiang   shang   anzhuang   zhe.
          at   wall   on   install   ASP

   i) 'An air-conditioner is installed on the wall (*carelessly/*willingly).'
   ii) 'An air-conditioner is being installed on the wall (*carelessly/*willingly).'

   b. Kongtiao   (*yong   luosidao)
       air-conditioner   with   screwdriver
       zai   qiang   shang   anzhuang   zhe.
       at   wall   on   install   ASP

   i) 'An air-conditioner is installed on the wall (*with a screwdriver).'
   ii) 'An air-conditioner is being installed on the wall (*with a screwdriver).'

   c. (*Wei-*le*   ganjue   nuanhuo,)[4]   kongtiao
       in order to feel   warm   air-conditioner
       zai   qiang   shang   anzhuang   zhe.
       at   wall   on   install   ASP

   i) 'An air-conditioner is installed on the wall (*in order to feel warm).'
   ii) 'An air-conditioner is being installed on the wall (*in order to feel warm).'

The agentivity tests become a bit complicated when they come across LoC examples, such as (149). It is true that the *-zhe* LoC counterparts of (148a/b/c) also fail to pass the three diagnostics (see (150a/b/c)). At first sight, this appears to adequately support the agentlessness of both the canonical order and *-zhe* LoC.

(149) Qiang   shang   anzhuang   zhe   kongtiao.
       wall   on   install   ASP   air-conditioner

   i) 'On the wall is installed an air-conditioner.'
   ii) % 'On the wall an air-conditioner is being installed.'

(150) a. Qiang   shang   (*xinbuzaiyande/   *xinganqingyuande)
          wall   on   carelessly   willingly
          anzhuang zhe   kongtiao
          install   ASP   air-conditioner

   i) 'On the wall is installed an air-conditioner (*carelessly/*willingly).'
   ii) % 'on the wall an air-conditioner is being installed (*carelessly/*willingly).'

   b. Qiang   shang   (*yong   luosidao)
       wall   on   with   screwdriver
       anzhuang zhe   kongtiao.
       install   ASP   air-conditioner

---

[4] I chose this clause on purpose to avoid S-control reading, which I will come back to in the next chapter when dealing with the agentlessness in *-le* LoC.

3.2 Basic Facts About LoC and -zhe   59

i) 'On the wall is installed an air-conditioner (*with a screwdriver).'
ii) % 'On the wall an air-conditioner is being installed (*with a screwdriver).'

c. (*Wei-*le* ganjue nuanhuo,) qiang shang
   in order to feel warm wall on
   anzhuang zhe kongtiao
   install ASP air-conditioner
   i) 'On the wall is installed an air-conditioner (*in order to feel warm).'
   ii)% 'On the wall an air-conditioner is being installed (*in order to feel warm).'

However, as suggested by Paul et al. (2019), some traditional agentivity diagnostics, such as the availability of agent-oriented modifiers, are incompatible with LoC regardless of whether an agent is present. This is supported by the fact that the three tests above are incompatible with (133a) but compatible with the canonical ordered variant of (133a), as shown in (151a/b/c) and (152a/b/c).

(151) a. Beimen shang (*xinbuzaiyande/ *xinganqingyuande)
         North.Gate on carelessly willingly
         shou zhe yige lian.
         guard ASP 1-CL company
         'At the North Gate a company keeps guard (*carelessly/*willingly).'

      b. Beimen shang (*yong qiang)
         North.Gate on with gun
         shou zhe yige lian.
         guard ASP 1-CL company
         'At the North Gate a company keeps guard (*with guns).'

      c. (*Wei-*le* ganjue anquan,) beimen shang
         in order to feel safe North.Gate on
         shou zhe yige lian.
         guard ASP 1-CL company
         'At the North Gate a company keeps guard (*in order to feel safe).'

(152) a. Yige lian (xinbuzaiyande/ xinganqingyuande)
         1-CL company carelessly willingly
         zai beimen shang shou zhe.
         at North.Gate on guard ASP
         'A company keeps guard at the North Gate (carelessly/willingly).'

      b. Yige lian (yong qiang)
         1-CL company with gun
         zai beimen shang shou zhe.
         at North.Gate on guard ASP
         'A company keeps guard at the North Gate (with guns).'

      c. (Wei-*le* ganjue anquan,) yige lian

	in order to	feel	safe		1-CL		company
	zai	beimen	shang		shou		zhe.
	at	North.Gate	on		guard		ASP

'A company keeps guard at the North Gate (in order to feel safe).'

Since *shou* 'guard' is unergative with its overt agent *a company* present, the incompatibility with the agentivity tests in (151) shows that the test can only support the agentlessness of the canonically ordered example in (147) but not of the LoC variant in (149). Whether (149) contains an implicit agent or not is thus hard to detect. That said, since canonically ordered sentences like (147) are clearly agentless, the simplest assumption is that the same is true of its LoC counterpart, and I will proceed on that basis.

The next question is therefore how the agentless *-zhe* sentences should be accounted for. There are two possible answers to this question that we need to consider: one is a zero-morphology account according to which, in Chinese, agentive verbs have a homophonous unaccusative form that inherently has no agent, and it is always this unaccusative form that appears in agentless *-zhe* sentences. This would be analogous to the transitive *lay* and the unaccusative *lie* in English. If there is an unaccusative *install* in Chinese that means a machine stays where it is supposed to, so it can work properly, then it is easy to see why these sentences do not allow any agents (see (125) and (126)), since English *lie* does not allow an agent either, as shown in (153).

(153) a. The stone lies/*lays on the ground.
      b. John *lay/laid the stone on the ground.

However, a proposal along these lines would predict that the agentless *-zhe* sentences must be semantically non-agentive. In other words, it should not presuppose any prior human actions, just like (153a) does not presuppose that anyone laid the stone on the ground. But this is not the case. (149) and (147) can hardly be semantically non-agentive, since there does not exist a context where a machine is installed on a wall but has never been installed by anyone. Furthermore, there is a pair of verbs in Chinese that can be used effectively to argue against the non-agentivity account. These are the agentive transitive *zhong* 'grow' in (154a) and the unaccusative *zhang* 'grow' in (154b). Both the transitive *zhong* and the unaccusative *zhang* are compatible with *-zhe*, as illustrated in (155) and (156).

(154) a. Zhangsan ba meigui zhong zai di shang.
         Zhangsan ba rose grow at earth on
         'Zhangsan grew the roses on the earth.'
      b. Meigui zhang zai di shang.
         rose grow at earth on

3.2 Basic Facts About LoC and -zhe   61

'The roses grow on the earth.'

(155) a. Di   shang   zhong   zhe   meigui.
         earth   on   grow   ASP   rose
         'On the earth are grown roses.'
      b. Di   shang   zhang   zhe   meigui.
         earth   on   grow   ASP   rose
         'On the earth grow roses.'

(156) a. Meigui   zai   di   shang   zhong   zhe.
         rose   at   earth   on   grow   ASP
         'Roses are grown on the earth.'
      b. Meigui   zai   di   shang   zhang   zhe.
         rose   at   earth   on   grow   ASP
         'Roses grow on the earth.'

If the zero-morphology account were correct, then *zhong* in (155a) and (156a) should be regarded as a homophonous unaccusative form of *zhong* in (154a). This unaccusative *zhong* is predicted to be non-agentive. As a result, (155a/155b) and (156a/156b) are expected to be semantically interchangeable. However, this prediction is false. As also reflected in the translations, (155a) and (156a) obligatorily presuppose a previous action of planting, while (155b) and (156b) do not presuppose any prior actions at all. This suggests that the zero-morphology account cannot be the right solution.

(155b) shows that *-zhe* LoC does not require a prior activity presupposition, which chimes with Hu (1995) and Djamouri and Paul's (2017) suggestion that *-le* LoC requires a previous human action while *-zhe* LoC does not. However, these authors do not discuss whether *-zhe* LoC allows such a prior activity or requires the absence of it. Based on the semantics of (149) and (155a), I argue that *-zhe* LoC does not require the absence of such an activity. Rather, it depends on whether the verb in *-zhe* LoC encodes an event of change or not. Thus, example (135) (repeated here as (157)) from Hu (1995) should receive an account in which the verb is treated as a state, similar to stative *hang* in English. I will come back to the difference between *-zhe* LoC and *-le* LoC in the next chapter.

(157) Shushao   shang   gua   *le/zhe   yilun   ming   yue.
      tree.top   on   hang   ASP   one-CL   bright   moon
      'The bright moon is hanging over the top of the tree.' (Hu 1995, 106)

We are now left with only one possible account for the agentless *-zhe* sentences, which is to assume that they are derived by agent omission. As shown in the meanings of (147/149) and (155a/156a), although the agentless *-zhe* sentences do not pass any agentivity tests and thus are grammatically non-agentive, semantically they still denote agentive events. This is reminiscent of agent omission with *-zai*. This similarity leads me to consider whether agent omission in these two structures can receive a unified account. Before approaching the analysis of *-zhe* LoC, I will give a short review of my account for agent omission with *-zai* in Chapter 2, so it will be easier to see how *-zhe* LoC and *-zai* can be accounted for in a similar way.

3.3 Developing the APCC

Although I have already proposed the APCC to account for the external argument omission phenomenon found in *-zai* examples in the previous chapter, I have not discussed why and how the APCC should be developed in a detailed manner. Since the reason why the APCC is adopted instead of the RPCC is the different pattern displayed by the *-zhe* examples, in this section it is the best timing to go through the proposal the APCC from the beginning to make clear (i) why the APCC replaces the RPCC in accounting for the cases marked by different aspectual markers and (ii) why the APCC is formulated the way that it is.

3.3.1 Agent Omission is Sensitive to Aspect

In the previous chapter, I proposed that agent omission with *-zai* is only possible when a verb can be used in a delegation setting. Indeed, following agent omission, the sentence must be understood as involving delegation. This is illustrated in (158).

(158) a. Lisi   zai   anzhuang   kongtiao.
         Lisi   zai   install   air-conditioner
         i) 'Lisi is installing the air-conditioner.'
         ii) 'Lisi is having someone install the air-conditioner.'
     b. Kongtiao   zai   anzhuang.
         air-conditioner   zai   install
         'The air-conditioner is being installed.'
         Lit: 'the air-conditioner is installing.'

To account for the connection between agent omission and the delegation context in (158), I explored the possibility of adopting the Proper Containment Condition (PCC) proposed by Rappaport Hovav and Levin (2012) (the PCC is given in (159)). Since the original PCC proved inadequate to capture the delegation case in Chinese, I proposed a modified version that is able to account for both the English and Chinese data (the revised PCC is given in (160); see the discussion in Sect. 2.3).

3.3 Developing the APCC

(159) The Proper Containment Condition: When a change of state is properly contained within a causing act, the argument representing that act must be expressed in the same clause as the verb describing the change of state. (Rappaport Hovav and Levin 2012, 173)

(160) Revised PCC (RPCC): an external argument cannot be omitted if the event in which it is a participant overlaps with the verb's event of change.

The RPCC looks at 'overlapping events' in the entire runtime of events. It successfully captures the -*zai* cases in (158a)/(158b), but comes across problems when dealing with other aspectual variants. In particular, since the RPCC does not relate agent omission to aspect, it predicts that in all the aspectual variants of (158a)/(158b), agent omission should similarly be only allowed when the external argument is interpreted as a delegator. However, in (147) and (149) (repeated as (161) and (162)), *anzhuang* 'install' combines with -*zhe* and obtains either a stative reading or a progressive reading. In the stative reading, there is no problem for the utterer to be the person who installed the air-conditioner, but the progressive reading has the same requirement as the -*zai* cases in (158a)/(158b). In other words, agent omission in (161) and (162) is permitted even in the non-delegation context with the stative reading, but only permitted in the delegation context with the progressive reading. Moreover, the agentive counterparts in (163) and (164) show that the progressive reading yielded by -*zhe* behaves (at least marginally) similar to the -*zai* counterparts, since they both allow the external arguments to be projected; but the stative reading of -*zhe* displays a completely different pattern: here the projection of the external argument is blocked completely. The contrast between (158b) and (161)/(162) thus cannot be captured by the RPCC.

(161) Kongtiao   zai   qiang   shang   anzhuang   zhe.
       air-conditioner at   wall   on   install   ASP
       i) 'On the wall is installed an air-conditioner.'
       ii) 'An air-conditioner is being installed on the wall.'

(162) Qiang   shang   anzhuang   zhe   kongtiao.
       wall   on   install   ASP   air-conditioner
       i) 'On the wall is installed an air-conditioner.'
       ii) % 'On the wall an air-conditioner is being installed.'

(163) %[a]/*Qiang   shang   Zhangsan   anzhuang zhe   kongtiao.
       wall   on   Zhangsan   install   ASP   air-conditioner
       Marginally acceptable: 'on the wall Zhangsan is installing an air-conditioner.'
       not: 'on the wall is installed an air-conditioner as a result of Zhangsan installing it.'

(164) %/*Zhangsan   zai   qiang   shang   anzhuang   zhe   kongtiao.
       Zhangsan   at   wall   on   install   ASP   air-conditioner
       Marginally acceptable: 'on the wall Zhangsan is installing an air-conditioner.'
       not: 'on the wall is installed an air-conditioner as a result of Zhangsan installing it.'

[a] As I have covered in Footnote.4, (163) and (164) are marginally acceptable in the progressive interpretation but not in the stative interpretation

This issue can be successfully addressed by adopting a version of the PCC that looks at whether the referent of external argument is active *in the interval denoted by aspect*. This has the potential to solve the problem presented by examples like (161) and (162), since *-zhe* is compatible with placing TT in the target phase (the resultant state) and the agent is of course no longer active in that phase. This idea is formalized in the following aspectual version of the PCC:

(165)   The Aspectual Proper Containment Condition (APCC—draft version)
        In order for an external argument to be eliminated, it should not participate in the event denoted by the predicate in the interval specified by aspect.

As in the previous chapter, I will present diagrams that show the alignment between three tiers. At the top, I show the arrangement of events in the mental model. In the middle, I show how the runtime of the event denoted by the verb is aligned with the events in the mental model. Finally, at the bottom, I show how the Topic Time (TT) is aligned with the runtime of the verb's event variable. In these diagrams, e_D represents an event of delegation and e_1 a causing event. e_2 is a become event and e_s represents the result state in which it culminates.[5] X represents the agent, Y is the theme, and D the delegate. If D is shown italicised, it is not a candidate for projection into the syntax. Rather we are concerned with establishing whether X is projected or not.

Consider first diagram (166) for example (158a)/(158b). In the delegation context, the event of delegation e_D precedes the causing event e_1. X represents the delegator, who delegates the task to a delegate D, and the actions of this unprojected D cause the becoming installed of the air-conditioner. Since TT aligns within the source phase of T-SIT, it is possible for TT to stay within the span of e_1 and so it does not overlap with e_D at all, as shown in (166). As a result, X does not have to participate during the interval of TT. (166) thus successfully predicts that the agent-omitted example (158b) is felicitous in the delegation context.

(166)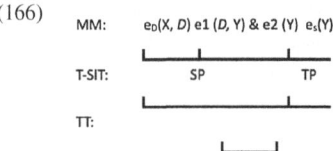

Now the question is why the stative reading of (161) and (162) does not require a delegation context like (158b) does. Since the examples allow the stative reading, *-zhe* can place TT in the target phase, which represents the result state. The relevant alignment is shown in (167). In the non-delegation context, the agent X participates in the installing event which causes the overlapping event of the air-conditioner

---

[5] The event structure of an accomplishment that I adopt here is a simplified version of Rothstein (2012), who proposes that an accomplishment contains an activity e_1, a become event e_2 and an incremental chain that relates e_1 and e_2.

3.3 Developing the APCC   65

becoming installed. Since TT must stay in the target phase but the participation of X only takes place in the span of the source phase, there are no actions of X during TT and therefore the APCC allows omission of X. In sum, the omission of the agent in (161)/(162) is possible even in a non-delegation context.

(167)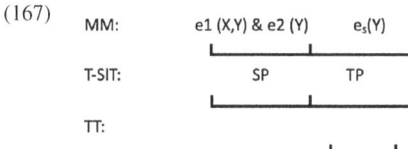

Of course these examples are not incompatible with the delegation context. This is easily seen in (168), where again X is not active in the interval specified by TT. We may conclude that agent omission in (161/162) is possible in any context, whether delegation is involved or not.

(168)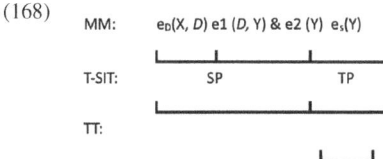

The APCC also predicts that the agent omission in (161) and (162) is not sensitive to the delegation context only in the stative reading. The progressive reading of (161) (and marginally (162)) is predicted to require a context of delegation, exactly as with the *-zai* counterparts represented in (166). This prediction is also borne out, since the progressive reading with the agent omitted is inappropriate if the speaker is the person who is installing the air-conditioner.

3.3.2 Agent Omission Is Obligatory

As I have shown, the APCC easily captures the fact that two-phase agentive verbs can occur with *-zhe* without realising their external arguments and obtain a stative reading. This is the case where *-zhe* locates TT within the target phase of T-SIT, which is a result state. External arguments naturally do not participate in that state and therefore the condition for agent omission is met. This is illustrated in (169).

(169)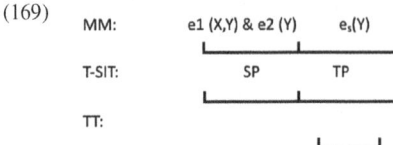

The APCC as it stands *allows* agent omission under these conditions, but we should ask whether it should instead not be *required*. This is an important question: if it is required, then it is easy to see why agentless stative *-zhe* sentences like (123) and (124) do not allow agents at all. The stative reading requires alignment of TT somewhere in the target phase and so X will never have actions in this interval. However, *-zai* sentences with a delegation context can occur with or without an agent (exemplified in (158a/158b)), which seems to suggest that agent omission is optional. Nevertheless, as I will now argue, the cases discussed so far allow us to adopt the stronger version of the APCC, which says that when the right conditions are met, agent omission is obligatory.

The key point is that the fact that *-zai* sentences in a delegation setting can keep an agent is already readily accounted for, given that TT can differ in size and temporal location. Suppose first that TT is small enough to be contained properly in the causing act and does not overlap with the delegation event. On this alignment, the agent, which only participates in the delegation event, shows no participation in the interval of TT. Assume that therefore it must be omitted. This is shown in (170). The diagram in (171) captures the alternative case, where TT is positioned in such a way as to overlap with the delegation event. Since in that case the agent participates in the interval of TT, it cannot be eliminated.

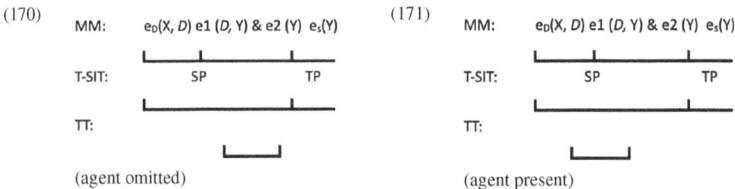

We can therefore strengthen the APCC as follows:

(172) APCC (final version): An external argument is eliminated if and only if its referent does not participate in the eventuality denoted by the predicate in the interval yielded by aspect.

In this section, I have proposed the APCC and shown that it not only explains the data that the PCC/RPCC accounts for, but also solves problems that the PCC/RPCC fails to deal with. It remains to be shown how the APCC captures the data for the full range of verb types. In the following part, I will go through the combinations of

3.4 Accounting for the Data with the APCC

different types of verbs with -*zhe* in both the canonical ordered sentences and LoC, to investigate whether they disallow, allow or force agent omission and show that the APCC can capture the different cases successfully.

3.4 Accounting for the Data with the APCC

3.4.1 1-Phase Verbs

When -*zhe* combines with activities, it receives a progressive reading rather than a result state reading. This is captured by the definition I propose for -*zhe*, which says that TT aligns inside any phase of T-SIT. In the case of activities, TT locates within the only phase of T-SIT and thus yields the progressive reading, similar to -*zai*. (173) and (174) are two examples involving LoC and the canonical order, respectively.

(173) Kaoxiang li kao zhe dangao.
 oven in bake ASP cake
 'A cake is being baked in the oven.'
(174) Dangao zai kaoxiang li kao zhe.
 cake at oven in bake ASP
 'A cake is being baked in the oven.'

The selection of activities in the agentless -*zhe* sentences is quite restricted: they mainly denote events that take place automatically, i.e., they all need a context of delegation. This is predicted by the APCC, since without delegation it is impossible for the referent of the external argument to have no participation in the event during TT. The required alignment for omission is shown in (175). Since TT can be located anywhere in T-SIT, it is also predicted that activities should be compatible with an agent. The agent will be realised on the alignment shown in (176), where TT partly covers the delegation event. This prediction is borne out, as (177) and (178) both sound natural according to native speakers.

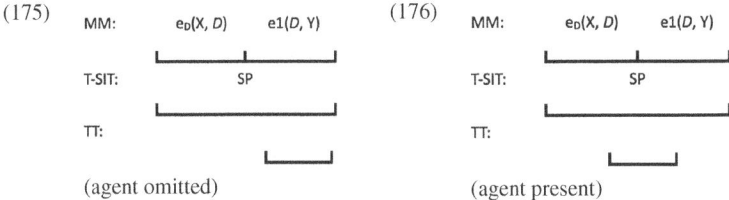

(177) Kaoxiang li wo kao zhe dangao (ne),
 oven in I bake ASP cake PAR
 xianzai bu neng dakai.
 now not can open
 'In the oven I'm baking a cake. It can't be opened now.'

(178) Wo zai kaoxiang li kao zhe dangao (ne),
 I at oven in bake ASP cake par
 xianzai bu neng dakai.
 now not can open
 'In the oven I'm baking a cake. It can't be opened now.'

The literature on -*zhe* LoC mainly focuses on accomplishments and seldom discusses activities. Based on the pattern of accomplishments in -*zhe* LoC, Pan (1996) claims that agents can never co-occur with -*zhe* LoC and further proposes that the absence of an agent results from agent deletion triggered particularly by -*zhe*. This may not be wrong within the scope of accomplishments, but if we also take activities into consideration, (177) presents a counterexample to Pan's claim and also challenges his -*zhe* deletion proposal, which predicts that no agent can occur in a -*zhe* LoC regardless of whether the verb is an accomplishment or an activity. Therefore, the contrast noted above between accomplishments and activities in the -*zhe* LoC cannot be captured. Instead, the proposal advanced here does not entail that -*zhe* triggers the removal of agents per se. Rather this depends on how TT aligns with T-SIT and how T-SIT is related to events in the mental model. What allows or disallows agent omission is whether these alignments satisfy the APCC.

For agent omission to occur in -*zhe*-marked activities, the presence of a delegation event is a requirement, since otherwise it will not be possible to locate TT in such a way that it does not cover any activities of this argument (see (175)). In other words, the APCC predicts that the agent of an activity marked by -*zhe* cannot be omitted in a non-delegation context, which is borne out. In Chinese, *kao* can mean either 'bake' or 'grill', and the meaning of 'grill' is incompatible with a delegation context since it needs the person who grills to hold the kebabs and keep turning them around.[6] Hence, (179a) and (180a) cannot undergo agent omission.

(179) a. Luzi shang Zhangsan kao zhe rouchuan.
  grill on Zhangsan grill ASP kebabs
  'On the grill Zhangsan is grilling kebabs.'
 b. *Luzi shang kao zhe rouchuan.
  grill on grill ASP kebabs

---

[6] If the grill is automatic and thus does not need a person to always hold the kebabs, (179b) and (180b) can be acceptable, but note that in that case it is the delegation reading again and the APCC thus still makes the correct predictions.

3.4 Accounting for the Data with the APCC   69

Intended meaning: 'on the grill someone is grilling kebabs.'

(180) a. Zhangsan zai luzi shang kao zhe rouchuan.
      Zhangsan at grill on grill ASP kebabs
      'Zhangsan is grilling kebabs on the grill.'
    b. *Rouchuan zai luzi shang kao zhe.
       kebabs at grill on grill ASP
       Intended meaning: 'kebabs are being grilled on the grill.'

That the agents in (179a) and (180a) are obligatorily present follows from the alignment shown in (181):

(181)   MM: e1(X,Y)
               └────┘
        T-SIT: SP
               └────────┘
        TT:
               └─────┘

The case of activities challenges another generalisation of Pan's, namely that a verb occurring in -*zhe* LoC must have a result state. Pan gives example (182) to support this claim, suggesting that *da* 'hit' does not have a result state. However, (173) has no result state either but is acceptable. This indicates that lacking a result state is not responsible for the ungrammaticality of (182).

(182) *Jia li da zhe Bill.
      home inside hit ASP Bill
      Lit: 'someone is beating Bill at home.'

I argue that (182) can be captured by the APCC, since *da* 'hit' is an activity that does not allow a context of delegation, as shown in (183).

(183) John zai da Bill.
      John ASP hit Bill
      'John is hitting Bill.'
      Not: 'John is having someone hit Bill.'

As a result, (182) must also be represented as in (181), where the external argument X has to participate in the interval of TT. Therefore, it is unsurprising that (182) is infelicitous.

The same logic is sufficient to answer the unsolved question that I brought up in Sect. 3.2, namely why unergative verbs in LoC -*zhe* cannot undergo agent omission. This was shown in (133a) and (134a), repeated here as (184a) and (184b). Their canonical ordered counterparts show the same pattern, which are shown in (185a) and (185b).

(184) a. Beimen   shang shou   zhe/le yige   lian.
       North.Gate on   guard ASP   1-CL   company
       'At the North Gate a company keeps guard.' (Paul et al. 2019, 30)
   b. *Beimen   shang shou   zhe/le.
       North.Gate on   guard ASP
       Intended meaning: 'At the North Gate someone keeps guard.'

(185) a. Yige   lian   zai   beimen   shang shou   zhe.
       1-CL   company at   North.Gate on   guard ASP
       'A company keeps guard at the North Gate.'
   b. *Zai   beimen   shang shou   zhe.
       at   North.Gate on   guard ASP
       Intended meaning: 'someone keeps guard at the North Gate.'

Shou 'keeping guard' is also an activity incompatible with a delegation context. Therefore, it should also be analysed as in (181), so that the obligatory participation of the external argument X in the predicated event during TT explains the infelicity of (184b) and (185b). For the same reason, (186) cannot undergo agent omission either, as shown in (187).

(186) Shibing   zai   shou   beimen.
      soldiers ASP   guard   North.Gate
      'The soldiers are keeping guard at the North Gate.'
      Not: 'The soldiers are having someone keep guard at the North Gate.'
(187) *Beimen   zai   shou.
       North.Gate ASP   guard
       Not: 'the North Gate is being guarded.'

That unergatives disallows a delegation context is not surprising. Hale and Keyser (1993) propose that initial lexical projection of unergatives consists of a light verb and a nominal complement, which then undergoes incorporation to form a verb. The light verb *v* has different forms such as *do*, *get* or *make*, and in the case of unergatives the light verb is *do*. Based on this suggestion, *guard* has the underlying structure [*do* guard]. Since this light verb can only select doers but not delegators, it is expected that unergatives are incompatible with a delegation context. As a result, they cannot undergo agent omission.

-Zhe can also combine with states and of course obtains a stative reading. For example:

3.4 Accounting for the Data with the APCC 71

(188) Zhangsan   ai   zhe   qizi.
       Zhangsan   love   ASP   wife
       'Zhangsan loves his wife.'

Yeh (1993) and Smith (1997) suggest that *-zhe* can only combine with stage-*le*vel states but not individual-*le*vel states, which is shown in (189). Yeh (1993) attributes this selection to the fact that stage-*le*vel states 'have a potential for change', while individual-*le*vel states do not (86).

(189) *Ta   conghui   zhe.
       he   intelligent   ASP
       Intended meaning: 'He is intelligent.'
       (Smith 1997, 274)

Klein et al. (2000) treat individual-*le*vel states as 0-phase predicates and stage-*le*vel states as 1-phase predicates. This is enough to account for the contrast between (188) and (189), since it is not possible to locate TT in a 0-phase predicate.

(188) has the representation in (190), where TT locates within the only phase of T-SIT and yields a stative reading. As the alignments show, the external argument X has to participate in the eventuality during TT, so the APCC predicts that X can never be omitted. This is borne out, as shown in (191).

(190)   MM: e1(X,Y)
                    └─────┘
        T-SIT: SP
                    └─────┘
        TT:
                      └───┘

(191) *Qizi   ai   zhe.
       wife   love   ASP
       Intended: 'the wife is loved.'

Among the states that can combine with *-zhe*, the posture states such as *stand* and *sit* are available in *-zhe* LoC. They are also represented by (190) and predicted by the APCC to be incompatible to agent omission, and again this prediction is correct.

(192) Yizi   shang   zuo   zhe   yige   haizi.
       chair   on   sit   ASP   one-CL   child
       'On the chair is sitting a child.'

(193) *Yizi   shang   zuo   zhe.
       chair   on   sit   ASP
       Intended meaning: 'on the chair is sitting someone.'

3.4.2 2-Phase Verbs

The combination of *-zhe* and telic predicates leads to more complex situations. As I have covered previously, for 2-phase verbs, *-zhe* can align TT within either the source phase or the target phase of T-SIT, yielding the progressive reading or the stative reading.

(194) and (195) show the two readings of *-zhe*. (194) allows the lexicalised agent and only has a progressive reading, while the agentless (195) obtains a stative reading. However, (195) is not incompatible with a progressive reading. Although the agentless *-zhe* with the progressive reading sounds less natural to native speakers' ears, with the proper context, (196) is regarded by most speakers as an acceptable sentence.

(194) | Zhangsan | zai | qiang | shang | anzhuang | zhe | kongtiao.
| | Zhangsan | at | wall | on | install | ASP | air-conditioner

'Zhangsan is installing an air-conditioner on the wall.'
Not: 'an air-conditioner is installed on the wall as a result of Zhangsan installing it.'

(195) | Kongtiao | zai | qiang | shang | anzhuang | zhe.
| | air-conditioner | at | wall | on | install | ASP

i) 'On the wall is installed an air-conditioner.'
ii) 'An air-conditioner is being installed on the wall.'

(196) | Kongtiao | hai | zai | qiang | shang | anzhuang | zhe,
| | air-conditioner | still | at | wall | on | install | ASP
| | fangdong | jiu | congcongde | zou | le
| | landlord | just | hastily | leave | ASP

'While the air-conditioner was still being installed on the wall, the landlord left hastily.'

Anzhuang 'install' is representative as an accomplishment verb that allows the context of delegation. The canonically ordered examples above show the pattern that when the agent is projected, the progressive reading is available but the stative reading is not. Contrastively, when the agent is absent, both readings are okay. Native speakers do not agree on the question whether LoC behaves similarly. It is agreed that the stative reading is incompatible with the agentive LoC and compatible with the agentless LoC, which is shown in (197) and (198). However, as regard to whether they can have the progressive reading, there are different views. With the same context as in (196), the progressive examples (199) and (200) are accepted by some speakers but rejected by others. In other words, LoC has the same pattern with the canonically ordered *-zhe* sentences in the judgements of some native speakers but not all.

3.4 Accounting for the Data with the APCC

(197) #Qiang shang Zhangsan anzhuang zhe kongtiao.
 wall on Zhangsan install ASP air-conditioner
 Intended meaning: 'on the wall there is an air-conditioner installed by Zhangsan.'

(198) Qiang shang anzhuang zhe kongtiao.
 wall on install ASP air-conditioner
 'On the wall is installed an air-conditioner.'

(199) ?Qiang shang hai anzhuang zhe kongtiao,
 wall on still install ASP air-conditioner
 fangdong jiu congcongde zou le
 landlord just hastily leave ASP
 'While the air-conditioner was still being installed on the wall, the landlord left hastily.'

(200) ?Qiang shang Zhangsan hai anzhuang zhe kongtiao,
 wall on Zhangsan still install ASP air-conditioner
 fangdong jiu congcongde zou le
 landlord just hastily leave ASP
 'While Zhangsan was still installing the air-conditioner on the wall, the landlord left hastily.'

The following diagrams shows how the pattern found in the canonical ordered sentences and marginally in LoC can be captured by the APCC. For such an accomplishment with the delegation context, the mental model contains the delegating event e_D, the installing event e_1, the becoming installed event e_2 and the result state e_s. e_D occurs first, which has two arguments, namely the delegator X and the unprojected delegate D. e_1 and e_2 take place simultaneously, followed by the result state e_s that the air-conditioner is installed on the wall. The running times of e_D, e_1 and e_2 constitute the source phase in T-SIT, while the time e_s holds is represented as the target phase. Given the definition of -*zhe*, TT can locate within SP or TP.

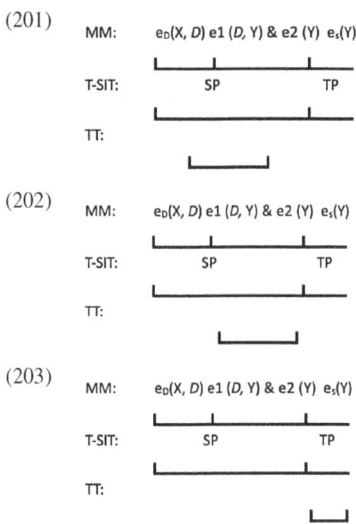

(201) and (202) show that when TT stays within SP, it can choose to overlap with e_D, where the agent X participates, or not to overlap with it. In the case of (201) where e_D overlaps with TT, the APCC predicts that the agent X has to be projected, while in (202), the APCC predicts that X must be eliminated as its participation does not overlap with TT at all. (203) is the case I have discussed in 3.3.3.2, in which TT locates in TP and can never overlap with e_D. Hence, the APCC predicts that the agent cannot be realised at all. In sum, in the progressive reading, the agent can be either present or omitted, while in the stative reading, the agent has to be omitted. This is exactly how the pattern appears in the examples above.

Admittedly, the APCC cannot explain the issue of why the progressive reading in LoC is not accepted by everyone. Although the issue does not challenge the APCC and may be subject to some particular mechanisms in LoC, what these exactly are is not clear yet and calls for further research.

So far, the APCC has accounted for *anzhuang* 'install' correctly, which is an accomplishment that permits the delegation context. However, there are also accomplishments that are incompatible with the delegation context, and they of course have

3.4 Accounting for the Data with the APCC

different mental models. So the next question is, does the APCC also capture these verbs successfully?

I choose the verb *hua* 'draw' to represent this type of verb. As (204) suggests, *hua* 'draw' does not allow the delegation context.

(204) Zhangsan zai hua xiangrikui.
Zhangsan ASP draw sunflower
'Zhangsan is drawing sunflowers.'
Not: 'Zhangsan is having someone draw sunflowers.'

Without the delegation event, the mental model of *hua* 'draw' only contains e_1, e_2 and e_s, with e_1 and e_2 taking place simultaneously. The progressive reading and the stative reading are illustrated in (205) and (206). When TT locates in SP and yields a progressive reading, TT inevitably overlaps with e_1, in which the agent X participates, and when TT locates in TP to trigger the stative reading, TT cannot overlap with e_1. As a result, the APCC predicts that the agent must be present in the progressive reading and omitted in the stative reading. Again, this is confirmed by the facts, as shown in (207)-(210).

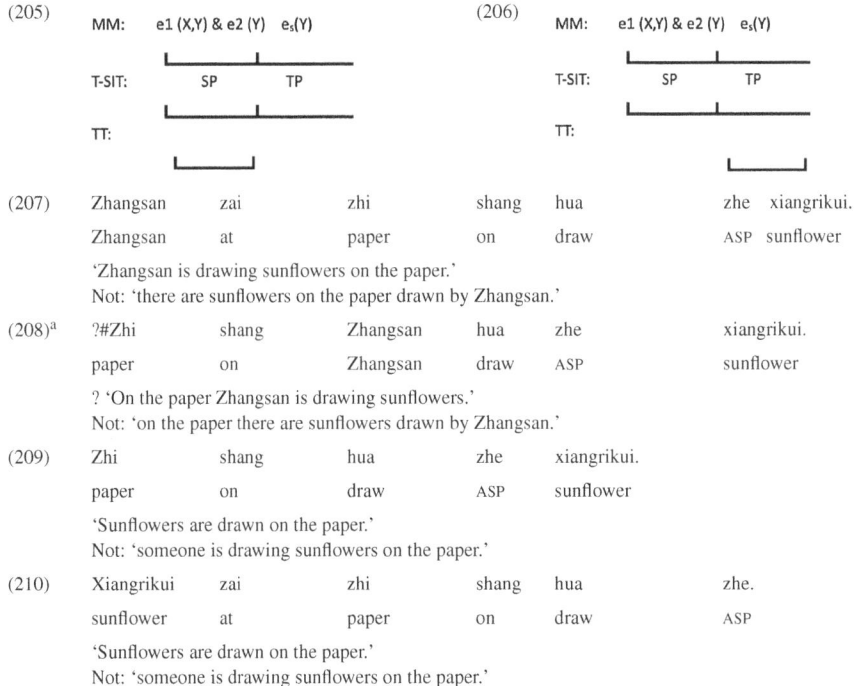

(207) Zhangsan zai zhi shang hua zhe xiangrikui.
Zhangsan at paper on draw ASP sunflower
'Zhangsan is drawing sunflowers on the paper.'
Not: 'there are sunflowers on the paper drawn by Zhangsan.'

(208)[a] ?#Zhi shang Zhangsan hua zhe xiangrikui.
paper on Zhangsan draw ASP sunflower
? 'On the paper Zhangsan is drawing sunflowers.'
Not: 'on the paper there are sunflowers drawn by Zhangsan.'

(209) Zhi shang hua zhe xiangrikui.
paper on draw ASP sunflower
'Sunflowers are drawn on the paper.'
Not: 'someone is drawing sunflowers on the paper.'

(210) Xiangrikui zai zhi shang hua zhe.
sunflower at paper on draw ASP
'Sunflowers are drawn on the paper.'
Not: 'someone is drawing sunflowers on the paper.'

[a] Similar to (200), the progressive reading of this example is also regarded felicitous by some native speakers but not all, but the stative reading is not accepted by any speakers I interviewed

We can see that in all the cases above, when the agent is present, only the progressive reading is available, while when the stative reading is obtained, the agent must be eliminated. This matches some suggestions in the literature. Pan (1996, 427) claims 'a verb without agent is more stative than one with it'. Dai (1997, 90) suggests that with agents, *-zhe* sentences tend to be more dynamic, while without agent, *-zhe* sentences will be more stative. These suggestions capture some connections between the progressive/stative readings and agents, but they are not accurate in some situations. One counterexample is that an agent-omitted *-zhe* sentence can obtain the progressive reading if the verb allows delegation, which I investigated in 3.3.2.1. Next, I will approach a more complicated case: *kai* 'open', which is also a counterexample to the generalisations above, and I argue that the APCC can nevertheless capture it.

Similar to *hua* 'draw', *kai* 'open' does not have the delegation reading, which is shown in (211).

(211) Zhangsan   zai   kai   men.
      Zhangsan   ASP   open   door
      'Zhangsan is opening the door.'
      Not: 'Zhangsan is having someone open the door.'

However, *kai* 'open' seems to be different from *hua* 'draw' in that its become event e_2 is instantaneous (that is, it is an achievement). In other words, the door is considered open once it opens a little. Therefore, e_2 should be treated as a two-point interval, of which the initial point overlaps with the end point of e_1, and the end point overlaps with the initial point of e_s. This can be seen from the ungrammaticality of (212), where the unaccusative form of 'open' combines with the progressive *-zai*.

(212) *Men   zai   kai.
      door   ASP   open
      Intended meaning: 'the door is opening.'

If the become event in (212) were gradual, it would be possible for TT to locate within the become event to yield a progressive reading. But if the become event is considered instantaneous, then (212) can be captured, since TT cannot be located inside a two-point interval.

In the transitive case, if the door opened as Zhangsan kept pushing on it, the mental model of the verb will contain the pushing event e_1 and the become event e_2, followed by the result state e_s, with the instantaneous e_2 overlapping with the end point of e_1. Again, e_2 is too small for TT to be located in. Thus, as the alignments in (213) and (214) show, the APCC predict that the progressive reading with *-zhe* forces the agent to be projected while the stative reading with *-zhe* disallows it.

3.4 Accounting for the Data with the APCC

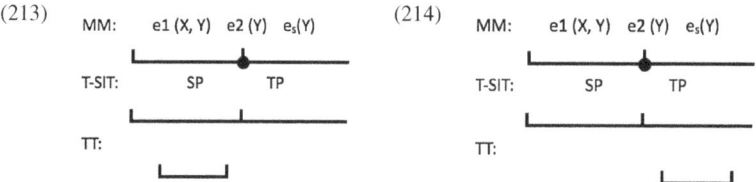

(213) (214)

This prediction is borne out, as shown in (215) and (216):

(215) Zhangsan kai zhe men.[a]
Zhangsan open ASP door
'Zhangsan is opening the door.'
Not: 'The door is open as a result of Zhangsan opening it.'

(216) Men kai zhe.
door open ASP
'The door is open.'
Not: 'The door is being opened by someone.'

[a] Again, this sentence is not very natural when used separately, but the following example is perfectly acceptable, according to several native speakers:

Zhangsan.	yibian.	kai.	zhe.	men,	yibian.	da.	dianhua.
Zhangsan.	one-side.	open.	ASP.	door.	one-side.	make.	phone call.

'Zhangsan is opening the door when making a phone call.'

However, the mental model in (213) and (214) is not the only possible mental model of *kai* 'open'. The activity that causes the door to open can also precede the become event. This is the situation where one makes an action on the door first (such as shooting a ball onto the door or pressing a button that controls an electronic door), and the door opened after the action finished. In the mental model, the instantaneous e_2 will follow the end point of e_1 immediately, so e_1 and e_2 do not overlap.

Under this context, the judgements of (215) and (216) are still the same, and this can be accounted for by the APCC, as shown in (217) and (218). Although the different mental models do not make a difference to the grammaticality of (215) and (216), it is still important to tease them apart, since they indeed lead to different results if the aspectual marker *-le* replaces *-zhe*, which I will discuss in the next chapter. The mental model of *open* in (217/218) is found not only in Mandarin Chinese, but also in English (see (219)). I will also come back to it in the next chapter.

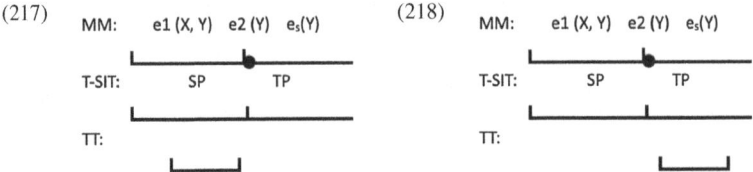

(219) Sally kept tugging on the door until it finally opened.

(Rappaport Hovav and Levin 2012, 23)

Moreover, the two mental models can also explain why (216) cannot obtain a progressive interpretation. Similar to (212), since e_2 is always a two-point interval, TT cannot locate within it no matter which mental model we consider it in.

Kai 'open' is also found with a different use, which is the maintenance reading, the reading that challenges Pan's (1996) and Dai's (1997) generalisations. The reading is illustrated in (220):

(220) Zhangsan   kai   zhe   men.
      Zhangsan   open   ASP   door
      'Zhangsan is keeping the door open.'

(220) can be used to depict a situation where the door has never been closed, and now it is Zhangsan who makes efforts to keep the door in an open state. In other words, Zhangsan did not cause a change of state. Instead, he is making contribution to maintaining a state. This is reminiscent of the stative use of causatives suggested by Kratzer (2000), exemplified in (221).

(221) Because of a congenital malformation, tissue obstructed the blood vessel.

(Kratzer 2000, 9)

Kratzer (2000) proposes that the stative use in (221) shows a causation relation between two states, while the eventive reading of causatives represents a causal relation between an event and a state. Therefore, what differentiates the stative use and the eventive use is whether the Davidsonian argument of the verb denotes a state or an event. The definition for the stative use does not fit (220), though, since (220) represents a causal relation between an event and a state.

3.4 Accounting for the Data with the APCC

Neeleman and van de Koot (2012) also investigate this phenomenon and refer to it as the maintenance use of causatives. They define the maintenance reading and give some English examples as follows:

(222) a. Maintenance is a relation between two eventualities: a maintaining state or event and a maintained state.
       b. Maintenance lacks a temporal dimension: the maintaining state or event must be contemporaneous with the maintained state.
       c. Maintenance is counterfactual: if the maintaining state or event were absent, the maintained state would not exist either. (Neeleman and van de Koot 2012, 39)

(223) a. The wall protects the city.
       b. John's uncle supports him financially.
       c. The beam carries the wall above it.
       d. The sheriff upholds the law. (Neeleman and van de Koot 2012, 39)

Neeleman and van de Koot (unpublished manuscript, 2016) suggest that the maintenance relation is an instance of the causal relation, and they define causation as (224):

(224) a. Causation is a relation between one or more causing eventualities and a caused eventuality.
       b. Causation obeys a temporal restriction: no causing eventuality may follow the caused eventuality.
       c. Causation is counterfactual: if the caused eventuality did not occur, then one of the causing eventualities did not occur either. (Neeleman and van de Koot 2016, 57)

The condition in (224b) that no causing eventuality may follow the caused eventuality covers both the ordinary causation, in which the caused event either precedes the causing event or overlaps with it, and maintenance, in which the maintaining state/event is simultaneous with the maintained state. In the case of (220), the event that Zhangsan keeps the door open and the opening state of the door are contemporaneous. Therefore, (220) has the diagram in (225):

(225)
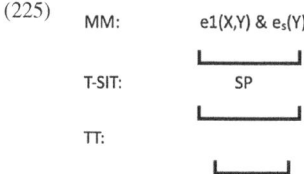

MM: e1(X,Y) & e$_s$(Y)

T-SIT: SP

TT:

As (225) shows, e_1 cannot avoid overlapping with TT, so the APCC predicts that (220) is incompatible with agent omission. This prediction is correct. Although the agentless counterpart is not an ungrammatical sentence, it is inappropriate in the context where someone keeps the door open.

(226) #Men   kai   zhe
      door   open   ASP
      Intended meaning: 'the door is kept opening by someone.'

In this section, I have shown that the APCC not only does not sacrifice any of the results obtained by the PCC proposed by Rappaport Hovav and Levin (2012), but also captures various cases concerning -*zhe* in Mandarin. In the next section, I will revisit some Chinese and English data from the perspective of the APCC, and show that the APCC can be applied to solve more puzzles cross-linguistically.

3.5 Conclusion

In this chapter, I have focused on absent agents with the imperfective marker -*zhe* in Chinese. I have argued that the agents do not exist either overtly or covertly in these cases, so the agentless -*zhe* sentences result from agent omission. Following the proposal of the APCC in the previous chapter, I argue that the APCC also accounts for the data marker by -*zhe*. Since the different patterns found between the -*zai* examples and the -*zhe* examples is the exact motivation for me to propose the APCC, through the analysis of the data, I have discussed how the APCC has been developed in a more detailed manner. The APCC predicts correctly when agents can (or must) be present and when they cannot in -*zhe* LoC as well as in canonically ordered sentences in which the verb is marked with -*zhe*.

References

Bresnan, J. 1994. Locative inversion and the architecture of universal grammar. *Language*: 72–131.
Bresnan, J., and J.M. Kanerva. 1989. Locative inversion in Chicheŵa: A case study of factorization in grammar. *Linguistic Inquiry*: 1–50.
Cornish, F. 2005. A cross-linguistic study of so-called "locative inversion": Evidence for the functional discourse grammar model. In *Morphosyntactic expression in functional grammar*, ed. C. de Groot and K. Hengeveld, 163–202. Berlin: Mouton de Gruyter.
Culicover, P.W., and R.D. Levine. 2001. Stylistic inversion in English: A reconsideration. *Natural Language & Linguistic Theory* 19 (2): 283–310.
Dai, Y. 1997. *Xiandaihanyushitixitongyanjiu* [A study on aspect in Mandarin Chinese]. Hangzhou: Zhejiang Education Press.
Djamouri, R., and W. Paul. 2017. A new approach to -zhe in Mandarin Chinese. In *Studies in Japanese and Korean historical and theoretical linguistics and beyond*, 110–123. Leiden: Brill.

References

Hale, K., and J. Keyser. 1993. On argument structure and the lexical expression of syntactic relations. In *The view from building 20: A Festschrift for Sylvain Bromberger*, ed. Hale and Keyser, 53–108. Cambridge: MIT Press.

Hu, W. 1995. Verbal Semantics of the Presentative Sentences. *Yuyanyanjiu* 2: 100–111.

Klein, W., P. Li, and H. Hendriks. 2000. Aspect and assertion in Mandarin Chinese. *Natural Language & Linguistic Theory* 18 (4): 723–770.

Kratzer, A. 2000. Building statives. Paper presented at the Annual Meeting of the Berkeley Linguistics Society.

Laws, J., and B. Yuan. 2010. Is the core-peripheral distinction for unaccusative verbs cross-linguistically consistent? Empirical evidence from Mandarin. *Chinese Language and Discourse* 1 (2): 220–263.

Levin, B., and M. Rappaport Hovav. 1995. *Unaccusativity: At the syntax-lexical semantics interface*. Cambridge: MIT Press.

Li, C.N., and S.A. Thompson. 1989. *Mandarin Chinese: A functional reference Grammar*. Berkeley and Los Angeles: University of California Press.

Liu, F.-H. 2007. Auxiliary selection in Chinese. In *Split auxiliary systems: A cross-linguistic perspective*, 181–205. Amsterdam: John Benjamins.

Lü, S. 1980. *XiandaiHanyuBabaiCi* [Eight hundred words of modern Chinese]. Beijing: The Commercial Press.

Neeleman, A., and H. van de Koot. 2012. The linguistic expression of causation. In *The theta system: Argument structure at the interface*, 37. Oxford: Oxford University Press.

Neeleman, A., and H. van de Koot, 2016. Unpublished manuscript, Department of Linguistics, University College London, London.

Pan, H. 1996. Imperfective aspect zhe, agent deletion, and locative inversion in Mandarin Chinese. *Natural Language and Linguistic Theory* 14 (2): 409–432.

Paul, W., Y. Lu, and T.H.-T. Lee. 2019. Existential and locative constructions in Mandarin Chinese. *The Linguistic Review* 37 (2): 231–267.

Rappaport Hovav, M., and B. Levin. 2012. Lexicon uniformity and the causative alternation. In *The Theta system: Argument structure at the interface*, 150–176. Oxford: Oxford University Press.

Rothstein, S. 2012. Another look at accomplishments and incrementality. In *Telicity, change, state: A cross-categorical view of event structure* (Oxford studies in theoretical linguistics), ed. V. Demonte and L. McNally, 60–102. Oxford: Oxford University Press.

Shan, C.-K., & B. Yuan. 2007. Is gradience of mapping between semantics and syntax possible in L2 acquisition. *BUCLD 31: Proceedings of the 31st annual Boston University Conference on Language Development*.

Smith, C. 1997. The aspectual system of Mandarin Chinese. In *The parameter of aspect*, 263–294. Berlin: Springer.

Yeh, M. 1993. The stative situation and the imperfective zhe in Mandarin. *Journal of Chinese Language Teachers Association* 28 (1): 69–98.

Open Access This chapter is licensed under the terms of the Creative Commons Attribution-NonCommercial-NoDerivatives 4.0 International License (http://creativecommons.org/licenses/by-nc-nd/4.0/), which permits any noncommercial use, sharing, distribution and reproduction in any medium or format, as long as you give appropriate credit to the original author(s) and the source, provide a link to the Creative Commons license and indicate if you modified the licensed material. You do not have permission under this license to share adapted material derived from this chapter or parts of it.

The images or other third party material in this chapter are included in the chapter's Creative Commons license, unless indicated otherwise in a credit line to the material. If material is not included in the chapter's Creative Commons license and your intended use is not permitted by statutory regulation or exceeds the permitted use, you will need to obtain permission directly from the copyright holder.

Chapter 4
Agent Omission with *-le*

Abstract This chapter captures the *-le* marked agent omission cases with the APCC. The aspectual marker *-le* is known for its complicated uses, and the author has proposed a general definition for *-le* that covers both the well-known perfective reading and the less-noticed stative reading. With the temporal alignments based on this definition, the APCC accounts for all the *-le* marked agent omission cases.

Keywords The stative reading of *-le* · Aspectual marker *-le*

4.1 Introduction

After accounting for agent omission with *-zai* and *-zhe* with the APCC, in this chapter, I will investigate sentences with *-le* and attempt to also capture the data with the APCC. Again, since the APCC relates the projection of the external argument to aspect, before the data analysis, the definition of *-le* under Klein et al.'s (2000) aspectual system needs to be determined. This definition may not be as easy to find as that of *-zai* and *-zhe*, since *-le* can yield both an eventive reading and a stative reading, which at first sight can hardly receive a unified account.

(227) Kongtiao   (ganggang/   xianzai)   anzhuang   le.
       air-conditioner just now   now   install   ASP
   i) 'The air-conditioner was installed (just now).'
   ii) 'The air-conditioner is installed (now).'

As shown in (227), the combination of *-le* and the VP 'installing the air-conditioner' denotes either a completed installing event (which occurred just now in the case at hand), or an installed state of the air-conditioner (which holds currently). Given these interpretations, the aspectual intervals must be represented as in (228) and (229), but what similarity the two readings have that makes them both marked by *-le* is a puzzle.

(228)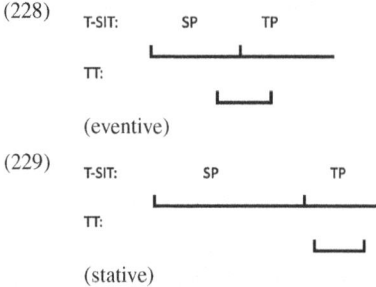

(eventive)

(229)

(stative)

In the eventive reading, TT obviously covers the end point of SP, which is a bound. I follow previous studies on -*le* (Hu 1995; Djamouri and Paul 2017) and argue that the stative reading of -*le* always presupposes a previous change-of-state event. I further argue that since a result state is homogeneous, this presupposition exists in every point of TP. If this presupposition is also treated as a type of bound, then the two readings can be captured in a unified way: -*le* requires that TT covers a bound.

In what follows I adopt this definition of -*le* when considering patterns of agent omission in -*le* sentences, with both the eventive reading and the stative reading. Agent omission is not only found with canonically ordered sentences with -*le*, but also with -*le* LoC, both of which I will study in the following section. I will show that the APCC makes correct predictions across the board, except for one case in -*le* LoC, which I attribute to an additional stativizing mechanism involved in LoC but not in canonically ordered sentences.

The phenomenon of agent omission with -*le* has been rarely investigated in the literature, but Tan (1991) threw some light on this topic. I revisit Tan's account for the data and suggest that although it can capture the data given in his thesis, it runs into problems when we consider aspectual variants of the examples. By contrast, I argue that the APCC can successfully capture the full set of the data.

After the data analysis, I turn to a comparison of stative sentences with -*zhe* and stative sentences with -*le*, which are regarded as semantically interchangeable in some—but crucially not all—contexts. Based on their different behaviours when combined with certain adverbials, I argue that stative -*zhe* is compatible with a prior change-of-state event but does not require it, while -*le* does.

The chapter is organised as follows. Section 4.2 is concerned with the eventive reading and the stative reading yielded by -*le*. Section 4.3 claims that agentless -*le* sentences result from agent omission and thus should be subject to the APCC. This section also proposes the unified definition of -*le* that covers both the stative and the eventive readings. I then consider agent omission in -*le* sentences and argue that the APCC captures these cases correctly. In Sect. 4.4, I review Tan's (1991) account and argue that the APCC does a better job accounting for the full range of data. Section 4.5 discusses the difference between stative -*zhe* and stative -*le*, while Sect. 4.6 concludes the chapter.

4.2 Discussions on -*le*

The definition and use of -*le* is presumably the most complicated among the four Chinese aspectual markers. In this section, I will firstly show the eventive/stative ambiguity found with -*le* and then suggest a unified definition of -*le* that covers both the eventive and the stative interpretation. I will also show through agentivity diagnostics that the apparently agentless cases marked by -*le* are truly agentless syntactically, in order to prepare for the coming analysis with the APCC on the -*le* cases.

4.2.1 The Eventive/Stative Ambiguity of -le

The aspectual marker -*le* has been widely discussed in the literature. Most researchers agree that -*le* gives rise to a change of state (CoS) reading when it combines with stative predicates (Li & Thompson 1989; Shi 1990; Ross 1995; Smith 1997; Klein et al. 2000; Lin 2003, among others). This is shown in (230). It marks the completion of an event of door opening followed by the result state of the door being open.

(230) Men   kai   le.[a]
       door   open   ASP
       'The door opened.'

[a]Since -*le* in examples like (230) is both verb-final and sentence-final, there are disagreements on whether it is an instance of verbal -*le* or sentential -*le*. I hold the view that it is verbal -*le* based on parallel data in Cantonese, where verbal -*le* and sentential -*le* are morphologically distinct (-*zo* for verbal -*le* and -*laa* for sentential -*le*). The Cantonese counterpart of (230) is only compatible with -*zo*.

mun.   hoi.   zo/*laa.
door.   open.   ASP/*PRT.
'The door has opened.'

However, I show that besides the prominent CoS reading, -*le* can also yield a stative reading, which, as far as I know, has not drawn much attention in the literature. The stative reading is associated with examples like (230), which is therefore ambiguous (see (231)). The modifier *xianzai* 'now' is introduced to force the stative reading, since the eventive reading is perfective and thus incompatible with this modifier.

(231) Men   (xianzai)   kai   le,

	door	now	open	ASP					
	dan	wo	bu	zhidao	shi	shenme	shihou	kai	de.
	but	I	not	know	be	what	time	open	PRT

'The door is open(ed) now, but I don't know when it opened.'

The stative reading seems to be close to the reading yielded by the durative aspectual marker *zhe*. In fact, it is true that -*zhe* can replace -*le* in (231) without much difference in meaning.

(232) Men (xianzai) kai zhe,
door now open ASP
dan wo bu zhidao shi shenme shihou kai de.
but I not know be what time open PRT

'The door is open now, but I don't know when it opened.'

Nevertheless, although not shown in the translations above, these examples are not semantically equivalent, since (231) presupposes a previous door-opening event, while (232) does not. The presence/absence of a CoS presupposition in the two types of stative readings can be revealed in four tests.

Firstly, a denial of the previous CoS event is incompatible with the stative reading yielded by -*le*, while -*zhe* is not selective.

(233) a. #Men kai le, qishi ta conglai mei guan guo.
door open ASP in fact it ever not close ASP

'The door is open(ed) now. In fact, it has never closed.'

b. Men kai zhe, qishi ta conglai mei guan guo.
door open ASP in fact it ever not close ASP

'The door is open now. In fact, it has never closed.'

Secondly, this subtle difference in meaning can be shown more straightforwardly with predicates such as *huo* 'alive'. To be more specific, in the stative reading of (234a), there is a strong implication that John is alive as a result of resurrection. Contrastively, (234b) simply demonstrates that John is alive and does not imply any previous resurrection at all.

(234) a. John huo le.

4.2 Discussions on -le

    John alive ASP
   'John became alive/John is alive now.'
   (Implication: John used to be dead)
 b. John hai huo zhe.
   John still alive ASP
   'John is still alive.'
   (No implication that John was dead)

The presence/absence of a CoS presupposition with -le and -zhe has been discussed in the locative inversion structure. Hu (1995) and Djamouri and Paul (2017) suggest that in a locative inversion structure, although -le and -zhe are generally interchangeable, -le presupposes a previous CoS event while -zhe does not.

(235) Shushao shang gua *le/zhe yilun ming yue.
   tree.top on hang ASP one-CL bright moon
   'The bright moon is hanging over the top of the tree.'
(236) Shushao shang gua *le/zhe yipian yezi.
   tree.top on hang ASP one-CL leaf
   'A leaf is hanging on the top of the tree.'

Since the moon is hanging on the tree metaphorically rather than physically, and the leaf grows out on the branch spontaneously, no previous hanging event is involved. In these cases, -zhe is compatible while -le is not, which indicates that the stative reading found with -le requires such an event.

  Last but not least, the adverb yizhi 'the whole time' is impossible with any presupposition of a prior CoS event and thus only compatible with -zhe but not -le.

(237) a. *Men yizhi kai le.
     door the whole time open ASP
     'The door has been opened the whole time.'
   b. Men yizhi kai zhe.
     door the whole time open ASP
     'The door has been open the whole time.'

Therefore, in (230), the combination of -le and the verb kai 'open' receives both an eventive reading, on which it denotes a change of state, and a stative reading, on which it denotes a result state but presupposes a prior change-of-state event. This eventive/stative ambiguity is not only found when -le combines with unaccusatives like kai 'open'. In the previous chapters, I have discussed some agentive verbs in Mandarin that can undergo agent omission, and some of these agentless counterparts show the eventive/stative ambiguity as well.

(238) Kongtiao   (ganggang/ xianzai) anzhuang le
      air-conditioner just now   now   install   ASP
   i) 'The air-conditioner was installed (just now).'
   ii) 'The air-conditioner is installed (now).'

(238) is compatible with both the eventive reading and the stative reading, but this is not the case for all the agent-omitted examples with -le. For example, (239) is only found with the eventive reading.

(239) Dangao (ganggang/ *xianzai) kao   le.
      cake   just now   now   bake ASP
   'A cake was baked just now.'
   Not: 'a cake is baked now.'

Moreover, there are agentive verbs that resist agent omission, as shown in (240):

(240) *Lisi da   le.
      Lisi   beat ASP
   Intended meaning: 'Lisi was/is beaten.'

(238), (239) and (240) represent three different patterns found with the agentless counterparts. (238) has both the eventive reading and the stative reading, (239) the eventive reading but not the stative reading, while (240) does not allow either. However, interestingly, no matter whether these agentless counterparts are compatible with the stative reading or not, none of their transitive counterparts allow the stative reading when combined with -le.

(241) Zhangsan (ganggang/ *xianzai) anzhuang le   kongtiao.
      Zhangsan just now   now   install   ASP air-conditioner
   'Zhangsan installed an air-conditioner just now.'
   Not: 'there is now an air-conditioner installed by Zhangsan.'

(242) Zhangsan (ganggang/ *xianzai) kao   le   dangao.
      Zhangsan just now   now   bake ASP cake
   'Zhangsan baked a cake just now.'
   Not: 'there is now a cake baked by Zhangsan.'

(243) Zhangsan (ganggang/ *xianzai) da   le   Lisi.
      Zhangsan just now   now   beat ASP Lisi
   'Zhangsan beat Lisi just now.'
   Not: 'Lisi is now in a state of beaten because Zhangsan beat him.'

Therefore, we may wonder whether the grammaticality of all the cases above can be attributed to a unified account regarding agent omission. I argue that these cases can be accounted for by the APCC, which I will show in detail in the next section.

4.2 Discussions on -le

Other than the cases above, there is more data concerning agent omission and -le. These involve the locative inversion construction (LoC). I discussed -zhe LoC in Chapter 3, but LoC can also be realized with -le, which I will investigate in this chapter. Both (238) and (239) have -le LoC counterparts, as shown in (244) and (245):

(244) Qiang   shang (ganggang/ xianzai) anzhuang le   kongtiao.
      wall   on   just now   now   install   ASP   air-conditioner
      i) 'On the wall was just now installed an air-conditioner.'
      ii) 'On the wall is now installed an air-conditioner.'

(245) Kaoxiang li   (ganggang/ *xianzai) kao   le   dangao.
      oven   in   just now   now   bake   ASP   cake
      'In the oven was baked a cake just now.'
      Not: 'in the oven there is a baked cake now.'

(244) and (245) pattern with their canonically ordered counterparts in (238) and (239): (244) exhibits the eventive/stative ambiguity while (245) is compatible with the eventive reading only. This seems to suggest that -le LoC and canonically ordered -le sentences should receive the same account. However, although in (238) the projected agent blocks the stative reading, the -le LoC counterpart of (238) is compatible with it, which is shown in (246). This indicates that -le LoC also shows some idiosyncratic differences that may need a separate account.

(246) Qiang   shang Zhangsan (ganggang/ xianzai) anzhuang le   kongtiao.
      wall   on   Zhangsan   just now   now   install   ASP   air-conditioner
      i) "On the wall Zhangsan installed an air-conditioner."
      ii) 'On the wall there is now an air-conditioner installed by Zhangsan.'

In what follows, I will show that both the canonically ordered agentless -le sentences and the agentless -le LoC are the result of agent omission, and account for them with the APCC. As for the stative reading with an agent, I will attribute it to an additional stativizing mechanism operative in LoC but not in canonically ordered sentences.

4.2.2 A Unified Definition of -le

Since the APCC concerns the relation between the mental model and aspect based on Klein et al.'s (2000) aspectual system, we need to give a clear definition for stative -le, which in the best case should also apply to eventive -le.

Klein et al. (2000) define -le as in (247). Given this definition, the change-of-state reading found with 2-phase and 1-phase verbs can be represented as in the diagrams in (248) and (249).

(247)   -le   For 2-phase verbs: TT overlaps with the pre-time of TP and TP
              For 1-phase verbs: TT overlaps with the pre-time of T-SIT and T-SIT[a]

[a] As noted in the previous chapter, the original formulation of Klein et al.'s (2000) definition for -*zhe* concerns the Distinguished Phase (DP), which I have not adopted in this thesis. Klein et al. (2000, 754) originally define -*le* as 'TT overlapping pre-time of DP and DP

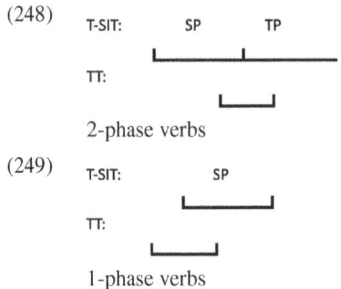

(248) 2-phase verbs

(249) 1-phase verbs

The definition for 2-phase verbs seems to successfully account for the eventive reading of (241) above, repeated here as (250). The VP 'air-conditioner installing' is 2-phased, containing an installation activity and a result state in which the air-conditioner is properly installed. (250) asserts that an installation activity took place and that this activity completed (so that the air-conditioner ended up in the installed state). It is therefore reasonable to assume that TT, the interval of assertion, overlaps with both SP and TP.

(250)   Zhangsan   (ganggang)   anzhuang   le   kongtiao.
        Zhangsan   just now   install   ASP   air-conditioner
        'Zhangsan installed an air-conditioner (just now).'

As for 1-phase verbs, Klein et al. (2000) argue that their definition captures examples like (251), in which 'fat' is a 1-phase stative verb, and TT covers both the pre-time of the fat state and the fat state to yield a change of state reading that 'she' was not fat and then became fat.

(251)   Ta   pang   le.
        she   fat   ASP
        'She became fat.' (Klein et al. 2000, 755)

4.2 Discussions on -le

It is true that (249) can capture (251) if the verb *pang* is treated as a stative verb. However, Klein et al.'s definition cannot apply to all the 1-phase verbs. For instance, it cannot explain why (242) (repeated as (252)) has a perfective reading rather than an inchoative reading.

(252) Zhangsan   ganggang   kao   le   dangao.
       Zhangsan   just now   bake   ASP   cake
       'Zhangsan baked a cake just now.'
       Not: 'Zhangsan started to bake a cake just now.'

The VP 'bake a cake' is also 1-phase, so Klein et al.'s definition predicts that (252) is necessarily inchoative, which is incorrect. The perfective reading found in (252) will need the alignment shown in (253), but that is not what (247) yields for this example.

(253) T-SIT: SP
                   └──────┘
       TT:
                       └──────┘

This is not the only drawback of Klein et al.'s definition for *-le*. Although it accounts for the eventive reading of 2-phase verbs, it fails to capture the stative reading I discussed in Sect. 4.2. The examples are repeated as (254) and (255) for convenience.

(254) Men   (xianzai)   kai   le.
       door   now   open   ASP
       'The door is opened (now).'
(255) Kongtiao   (xianzai)   anzhuang   le.
       air-conditioner now   install   ASP
       'The air-conditioner is installed (now).'

As I have shown, on its stative reading, a *-le* sentence makes an assertion about a result state and presupposes a prior CoS event. Therefore, (254) and (255) should be represented by a diagram like (256).

(256) T-SIT: SP   TP
                   └────────────┘
       TT:
                               └──────┘

I aim to find an alternative definition for *-le* that is able to cover the perfective reading in (250) and (252), the inchoative reading in (251), and the stative reading in (254) and (255). But before proposing this new definition, I will argue that (251) is not an inchoative reading of a stative verb and should not be represented as (249). Klein et al. (2000) assume that *pang* in (251) is a stative verb that is equivalent to *be fat* in English, and the inchoative reading is yielded by the aspect per se. However, Sybesma (1997) (see also Tham 2012) observes that a verb like *pang* 'fat' is compatible with a CoS reading even if *-le* is absent.

(257)   Ta   hui   pang.
        3SG   will   fat
        'He/she will get fat.'
                (Sybesma 1997, 230)

Furthermore, *pang* can be modified by a manner adverb in the absence of *-le*.

(258)   pang   de   kuai
        fat   SUB   quickly
        'getting fat quickly'

As the CoS flavours of (257) and (258) cannot be attributed to *-le*, we are led to the alternative proposal that a CoS is always lexically encoded. This is the view held by Tham (2012), who suggests that there are separate but homophonous stative and CoS lexical items in Mandarin. If we assume that *pang* in (251) is a 2-phase CoS verb, which is the equivalent of *fatten* in English, the 'becoming fat' interpretation in (251) can be analysed as (248): SP represents the becoming fat event while TP is the fat state, and TT overlaps with both.

On this analysis, (251) is unified with (250) and (252), and henceforth I will refer to this reading as the eventive reading. The new definition for *-le* thus needs to cover both the eventive reading and the stative reading. The two variations of the eventive reading are shown in (248) and (253), and it appears straightforward that they both represent the cases where TT covers the end point of SP, but how can this definition share a property with the definition of the stative reading?

I argue that *-le* requires TT to cover a bound, but that there are different types of bound, which lead to the eventive reading and the stative reading. As discussed previously, stative *-le* differs from stative *-zhe* in that *-le* presupposes a prior CoS event while *-zhe* does not. Yet this difference is not reflected in the alignment in (256), since this alignment can represent both stative *-le* and stative *-zhe*. In order to highlight this difference, the presupposition should be represented in the alignment of stative *-le*:

4.2 Discussions on -le 93

(259)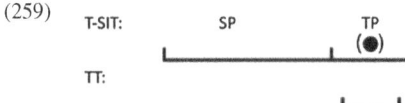

The dot in the brackets represents the presupposition of the previous change-of-state event. Since the result state (TP) is homogeneous, the event presupposition is found everywhere in TP. Therefore, if we treat this presupposition as a type of bound, the bound is covered by TT as long as any part of TP is covered by TT.

I thus propose that *-le* can be defined as (260).[1] In the eventive case, the bound is the end point of SP, while in the stative case it is the presupposition of the prior CoS event. This will explain why stative *-le* requires such a presupposition.

(260)   *-le*   TT covers a bound

4.2.3 No Implicit Agent with -le

As I have done in the previous chapters, before accounting for (238) as a case of agent omission, I will again apply agentivity diagnostics, including agent-oriented modifiers, instrument licensing and purpose clauses, to show that no implicit agent exists in (238).

---

[1] An alternative for the unified definition can be that TT covers the last phase of T-SIT with an additional CoS presupposition, and the distinction between the eventive reading and the stative reading is whether TT stretches to cover the boundary between SP and TP. This definition can yield similar results with the current definition, but I have not adopted it for two reasons.

First, the stipulation of the CoS presupposition is needed only for the stative reading and becomes a little redundant or even confusing in the eventive reading. Second, the temporal modifiers (e.g., *ganggang* 'just now', *xianzai* 'now', etc.) in Chinese always denote a time point in TT. As the translations of the examples above show, in the stative reading, the temporal modifier denotes a time point that can exist in any part of TP, while in the eventive reading, the temporal modifier always denotes the boundary between SP and TP. Since this alternative definition does not relate the definition of -le with the boundary between SP and TP, it cannot account for this pattern. Contrastively, in my current definition, it can be assumed that the temporal modifiers always denote the time of the bound that TT covers: in the eventive reading, it is the boundary separating SP and TP; while in the stative reading, it is the time of the presupposition—since the CoS presupposition exists everywhere in TP, it easily follows that the temporal modifier can denote any time point in TP.

(261) a. Kongtiao   (*xinbuzaiyande/ *xinganqingyuande) anzhuang le.
        air-conditioner carelessly   willingly   install   ASP
        i) 'An air-conditioner was installed (*carelessly/*willingly).'
        ii) 'An air-conditioner is installed (*carelessly/*willingly).'

      b. Kongtiao   (*yong luosidao)   anzhuang le.
         air-conditioner with   screwdriver install   ASP
         i) 'An air-conditioner was installed (*with a screwdriver).'
         ii) 'An air-conditioner is installed (*with a screwdriver).'

      c. (*Wei-le   ganjue nuanhuo,) kongtiao   anzhuang le.
         in order to feel   warm   air-conditioner install   ASP
         i) 'An air-conditioner was installed (*in order to feel warm).'
         ii) 'An air-conditioner is installed (*in order to feel warm).'

4.2 Discussions on -le

Based on the tests above, (238) does not have a covert agent, similar to its *-zai* and *-zhe* variants discussed in the previous chapters. Therefore, in the following part, I will treat examples like (238) as resulting from agent omission and explore their patterns.

The agentivity diagnostics become more complicated when it comes to the case of LoC. In the literature, there are views that *-le* LoC contains an implicit agent. Pan (1996) suggests that the agent in *-le* LoC is 'syntactically dropped' rather than deleted, based on the fact that an agent can be lexicalized in *-le* LoC but not in *-zhe* LoC. Paul et al. (2019) also agree that the agent in *-le* LoC is covertly present, and they give two pieces of evidence to support this idea. Firstly, following Hu's (1995) and Djamouri and Paul's (2017) arguments, they suggest that *-le* LoC presupposes a prior action of an agent, as discussed in Sect. 4.2. Example (235), repeated here for convenience as (262), shows that *-le* LoC requires such a prior action and thus is incompatible with a context where no such prior action exists.

(262) Shushao shang gua *le/zhe yilun ming yue.
 tree.top on hang ASP one-CL bright moon
 'The bright moon is hanging over the top of the tree.' (Hu 1995, 106)

This argument assumes that a semantically agentive verb must be grammatically agentive as well. This seems to be true in languages such as English and German, but is not necessarily the case in other languages. Bhatt (2009) and Bhatt and Embick (2017) propose that grammatical agentivity and encyclopaedic agentivity are independent from each other, and languages like Hindi-Urdu allow verbs to be encyclopaedically agentive while grammatically non-agentive. In Chapter 2, I followed and developed this idea and suggested that the possibility of agent omission is determined by the M parameter. I argued that Chinese is similar to Hindi-Urdu in the setting of this parameter, so it also allows verbs that are semantically agentive but grammatically non-agentive. Therefore, I take the view that the presupposition of a previous action of an agent in *-le* LoC is insufficient as evidence for an implicit agent.

Another piece of evidence that Paul et al. (2019) adduce is that *-le* LoC is compatible with purpose clauses and agent-oriented adverbials. The two examples they give are shown in (263) and (264).

(263) Weile   fangbian   duzhe   cankao,
      in.order.to facilitate   reader   consult
      Shu   hou   fu   le/*zhe[a]   xiangxi   de   shumu.
      book   after   add   ASP   detailed sub   bibliography

'In order to make it easier for the reader to consult (the book), at the end of book has been added a detailed bibliography.'

(264) Di   shang   buxiaoxin   sa   le/*zhe   hen
      ground   on   unintentionally spill   ASP   very
      duo   shui,   xingren   laiwang   dou
      much   water   passer.by   come.go   all
      bixu   shifen   dangxin
      must   very   careful

'On the ground has been unintentionally spilled a lot of water. All the passers-by have to be very careful.'
(Paul et al. 2019, 28)

[a] It should be clarified that the judgement that -zhe is incompatible here is from Paul et al. (2019) and does not represent the author's judgement. As a native speaker, I accept -zhe in this sentence. However, as I indicate in the following part, this test itself is not reliable since it has not considered the possibility of S-control. Therefore, no matter whether -zhe is possible in this example, it does not tell us much about agentivity.

4.2 Discussions on -*le*   97

However, these two tests are not as reliable as one would hope. Paul et al. (2019) attempt to show that (263) is grammatical because the PRO in the purpose clause is controlled by an implicit agent. However, there is another potential controller in this example, which is the matrix event. Williams (1974, 1985) and Lasnik (1988) propose that the matrix clause can be a controller, which is shown in (265):

(265)   The ship was sunk (by a torpedo) [PRO to prove a point]. (Lasnik 1988, 10)

Since it is pragmatically impossible for a torpedo to prove a point, the lexicalised agent in the by-phrase cannot be the controller. Instead, it is the event of the ship being sunk which controls the PRO. This phenomenon is named S-control by Lasnik (1988).

Now we can come back to (263). This example can also be accounted for if the matrix clause controls the PRO in the purpose clause. If so, it receives an interpretation that adding a detailed bibliography at the end of the book was intended to help the readers, which is a natural interpretation. When the purpose clause is S-controlled, the main clause can be a structure that definitely does not contain an agent, as shown in (266):

(266)   Weile   fangbian   duzhe   cankao,
        in.order.to facilitate   reader   consult
        shu   hou   you   xiangxi   de   shumu.
        book   after   have   detailed sub   bibliography
        'In order to make it easier for the reader to consult (the book), there is a detailed bibliography at the end of the book.'

As a result, (263) is not strong enough to support the presence of an implicit agent. In fact, we can reach a stronger conclusion: if we use other purpose clauses that cannot be controlled by an event, we get an unacceptable sentence. For example, a VP such as 'feeling warm' selects an experiencer as its external argument, which is [+m]. Hence an event cannot serve as the binder of such a PRO. The unacceptability of (267) with the purpose clause included therefore indicates that there is no hidden agent in the structure.

(267)   (*Wei-*le*   ganjue   nuanhuo,) qiang   shang   anzhuang   le   kongtiao.
        in order to   feel   warm   wall   on   install   ASP   air-conditioner
        'On the wall is installed an air-conditioner (*in order to feel warm).'

Contrastively, when the agent is present in -*le* LoC, the very same purpose clause is successfully licensed:

(268) (Wei-*le* ganjue nuanhuo,) qiang shang
in order to feel warm wall on
Zhangsan anzhuang le kongtiao
Zhangsan install ASP air-conditioner
'On the wall Zhangsan installed an air-conditioner in order to feel warm.'

These examples suggest that the purpose clause test in (263) is inadequate, and therefore the claim that apparently agentless *-le* LoCs contain a covert agent is debatable. Paul et al. (2019) also give (264) to support the presence of a covert agent. This example shows that *-le* LoC can contain the agent-oriented modifier 'unintentionally'. However, 'unintentionally' is not a good test for agentivity, as it is even compatible with unaccusative verbs that clearly have no causative counterparts. (269) shows one example, and (270) indicates that the verb compound 'flying away' has no causative use at all. This fact challenges the reliability of 'unintentionally' as evidence for an implicit agent.

(269) Qiqiu buxiaoxin fei zou le.
balloon unintentionally fly go ASP
'The balloon flew away unintentionally.'

(270) *Zhangsan fei zou le qiqiu.
Zhangsan fly go ASP balloon
Intended meaning: 'Zhangsan caused the balloon to fly away.'

Nevertheless, although I have shown that the evidence for an implicit agent in *-le* LoC provided by Paul et al. (2019) is not as convincing as it should be, the agentlessness of *-le* LoC is also not easy to prove. As I pointed out in the previous chapter when discussing the agentlessness of *-zhe* LoC, the structure of locative inversion is naturally incompatible with common agentivity diagnostics, even when the agent is projected (Tan 1991; Paul et al. 2019). For example, although (267) seems to suggest that *-le* LoC without the agent projected is truly agentless rather than having an implicit agent, the infelicity of (271) weakens the reliability of the test.

(271) (*Wei-*le* ganjue anquan,) beimen shang
in order to feel safe North.Gate on
shou le yige lian.
guard ASP 1-CL company
'At the North Gate a company keeps guard (*in order to feel safe).'

Therefore, for now we are unable to determine whether -*le* LoC has an implicit agent, since either side lacks convincing evidence, and whether there is an effective agentivity test for -*le* LoC needs further investigation. But again, as I claimed in the previous chapter, as we can confirm that canonically ordered sentences like (148) are indeed agentless, the simplest assumption is that the same applies to the -*le* LoC counterpart, and in what follows I will proceed on that basis.

4.3 Accounting for the Data with the APCC

In this section, I will investigate various cases of agent omission with -*le*, in both canonically ordered sentences and LoC, and show that the patterns can be captured by the APCC.

(272) APCC: An external argument is eliminated if and only if its referent does not participate in the eventuality denoted by the predicate in the interval yielded by aspect.

Similar to what I have done in the previous chapter, in the following part I will analyse the cases with diagrams showing temporal relations of three layers: the mental model, T-SIT and TT. The eventive reading and the stative reading of -*le*, as I just discussed, are represented by different alignments of T-SIT and TT. The eventive reading is found with both 1-phase verbs and 2-phase verbs, as shown in (273) and (274) respectively. The stative reading is only available for 2-phase verbs, which is illustrated in (275). That the stative reading is incompatible with 1-phase verbs follows from (260). On the stative reading TT anchors a prior CoS event presupposition in the result state. But since 1-phase verbs do not have a result state with such a presupposition, they also cannot have a stative reading.

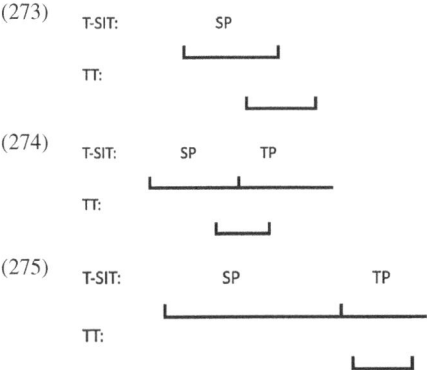

4.3.1 1-Phase Verbs

As shown above, 1-phase verbs are only compatible with the eventive reading and do not support a stative reading. Canonically ordered examples and LoC examples with such verbs are repeated as (276) and (277), respectively.

(276) Dangao   (ganggang/   *xianzai)   kao   le.
       cake   just now   now   bake   ASP
       'A cake was baked just now.'
       Not: 'a cake is baked now.'

(277) Kaoxiang   li   (ganggang/   *xianzai)   kao   le   dangao.
       oven   in   just now   now   bake   ASP   cake
       'In the oven was baked a cake just now.'
       Not: 'in the oven there is a baked cake now.'

The VPs in (276) and (277) denote an event that occurs automatically in the oven. In other words, these examples fit a delegation context. Therefore, the mental model will contain the event of delegation e_D and the causing event e_1. The external argument is the delegator X, who participates in e_D but not in e_1. The alignment is shown in (278).

(278)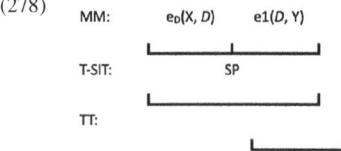

4.3 Accounting for the Data with the APCC   101

(278) shows why the agent omission in (276) and (277) is permitted by the APCC: when TT only overlaps with e_1 but not e_D, the external argument X does not participate in TT and thus is eliminated. However, TT can also stretch to overlap with both e_D and e_1, which predicts that the agent in (276) and (277) can also be projected. This prediction is borne out. The examples are given in (279) and (280) and the diagram in (281).

(279)   Zhangsan   kao   le   dangao.
        Zhangsan   bake   ASP   cake
        'Zhangsan baked a cake.'

(280)   Kaoxiang   li   Zhangsan   kao   le   dangao.
        oven   in   Zhangsan   bake   ASP   cake
        'In the oven Zhangsan baked a cake.'

(281)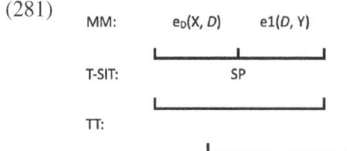

We can see that the flexibility of agent projection/omission above is because TT can alter its size to overlap with e_D or not overlap with it. This suggests that the event of delegation is significant for agent omission in this case. If there is no delegation context, the mental model will only contain e_1, in which the agent X participates. As a result, the agent will inevitably participate in TT. This alignment is shown in (282). Therefore, the APCC predicts that agent omission in 1-phase verbs will be blocked when used in situations that do not involve delegation. The data in in (283) and (284) corroborate this.

(282)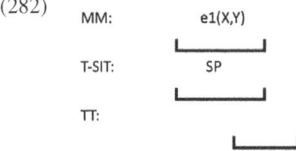

(283) a. Zhangsan kao le rouchuan.
 Zhangsan grill ASP kebabs
 'Zhangsan grilled kebabs.'
 b. *Rouchuan kao le.
 kebabs grill ASP
 Intended meaning: 'kebabs were grilled by someone.'
(284) a. Luzi shang Zhangsan kao le rouchuan.
 grill on Zhangsan grill ASP kebabs
 'On the grill Zhangsan grilled kebabs.'
 b. *Luzi shang kao le rouchuan.
 grill on grill ASP kebabs
 Intended meaning: 'on the grill someone grilled kebabs.'

As mentioned in the previous chapter, *kao* in Chinese can mean either 'bake' or 'grill'. In the meaning of 'bake', it seems that the delegation context is forced by the nature of this activity, since cake baking takes place automatically in an oven. Contrastively, for a verb like 'grill' the non-delegation context is forced, because kebab grilling needs a person to hold the kebabs over a grill, which cannot happen automatically. The data pattern in (283) and (284) shows that the APCC makes the correct prediction again. Without the event of delegation in the mental model, the participation time of the agent must overlap with TT, so that agent omission is impossible.

The alignment in (282) is also relevant for verbs that never allow agent omission with *-le*, such as *da* 'beat' in (240) (repeated as (285) here). Since the verb *da* is incompatible with a delegation context, the alignment in (282) is the only option for (285), thereby ruling it out. Since the agent participates in the event during TT, it must be projected.

(285) *Lisi da le.
 Lisi beat ASP
 Intended meaning: 'Lisi was/is beaten.'
(286) Zhangsan da le Lisi.
 Zhangsan beat ASP Lisi
 'Zhangsan beat Lisi.'

In the previous chapter, I also attempted to explain why unergative verbs in LoC cannot undergo agent omission, as exemplified in (287b). In the discussion, I showed why this is captured by the APCC in *-zhe* LoC, but did not cover the case of *-le* LoC. Here I argue that the *-le* LoC case is also successfully captured by the APCC: since *shou* 'keeping guard' is an activity incompatible with delegation, again the alignment in (282) is applicable. Therefore, the agent must participate in the aspectual interval and thus must be realised.

(287) a. Beimen   shang   shou   zhe/le   yige   lian.
          North.Gate   on   guard   ASP   1-CL   company
          'At the North Gate a company keeps guard.' (Paul et al. 2019, 30)
      b. *Beimen   shang   shou   zhe/le.
          North.Gate   on   guard   ASP
          Intended meaning: 'At the North Gate someone keeps guard.'

4.3.2 2-Phase Verbs

When 2-phase verbs combine with *-le*, as I have shown above, both the eventive reading and the stative reading may be available. In this section, I will discuss various cases of 2-phase verbs with *-le* and show that their patterns can be captured by the APCC.

First I return to the case of *anzhuang* 'install'. The examples given previously are repeated here as (288) and (289).

(288) Kongtiao   (ganggang/   xianzai)   anzhuang   le.
       air-conditioner   just now   now   install   ASP
       i) 'The air-conditioner was installed (just now).'
       ii) 'The air-conditioner is installed (now).'

(289) Zhangsan   (ganggang/   *xianzai) anzhuang   le   kongtiao.
       Zhangsan   just now   now   install   ASP   air-conditioner
       i) 'Zhangsan installed an air-conditioner.'
       ii) 'Zhangsan had an air-conditioner installed just now.'
       Not: 'there is now an air-conditioner installed by Zhangsan.'

(288) and (289) show that the agentless variant is compatible with both the eventive and the stative reading, while its transitive counterpart allows only the eventive reading. *Anzhuang* 'install' is a verb that permits a delegation context, as the translation of (289) suggests. In such a context, the mental model includes the event of delegation (preceding the causing event). Therefore, in such a context, the examples under discussion should be represented by the diagrams in (290), (291) and (292).

(290) illustrates the eventive reading of (288). The eventive *-le* requires TT to cover the end point of SP, but TT can alter its length to choose to overlap with e_D or not. In (290), TT does not overlap with e_D, in which the delegator D participates. Therefore, the APCC requires that the agent be eliminated on this alignment. Contrastively, if TT is long enough to overlap with e_D, we have (291). With this alignment, the APCC requires that the eventive reading with *-le* retains the agent. Taken together, we obtain precisely the optionality of agent omission illustrated by the pair of examples in (288) and (289).

In the stative reading shown in (292), TT stays within TP to cover the prior CoS event presupposition. On this alignment, TT does not overlap with e_D at all, so that the APCC predicts that the agent will have to be omitted. This is also confirmed, since the stative reading is only found with (288) but not with (289).

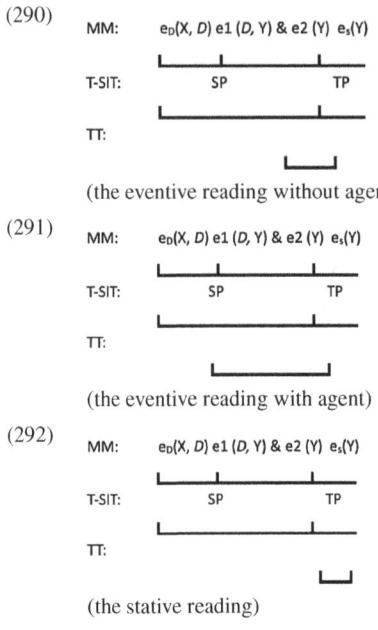

(290) (the eventive reading without agent)

(291) (the eventive reading with agent)

(292) (the stative reading)

Anzhuang 'install' represents the 2-phase verbs compatible with delegation, but there are also 2-phase verbs that are incompatible with a delegation context. An example is *hua* 'draw'. I discussed this case with *-zhe* in the previous chapter, and here I will investigate its interaction with *-le*.

(293) Zhangsan (ganggang/ *xianzai) hua le xiangrikui.
 Zhangsan just now now draw ASP sunflower
 'Zhangsan drew sunflowers (just now).'
 Not: 'there are sunflowers drawn by Zhangsan (now)'

(294) Xiangrikui (*ganggang/ xianzai) hua le.
 sunflower just now now draw ASP
 'Sunflowers are drawn (now).'
 Not: 'someone drew sunflowers (just now).'

4.3 Accounting for the Data with the APCC

As (293) and (294) indicate, the transitive variant only has the eventive reading while the agentless variant only has the stative reading. Since *hua* 'draw' does not allow a delegation context, its mental model only contains the causing event e_1, the become event e_2 and the result state e_s. e_1 and e_2 occur simultaneously. The alignments are shown in the following diagrams.

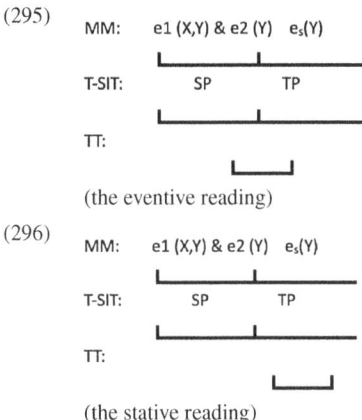

(295)

(the eventive reading)

(296)

(the stative reading)

On the eventive reading of *-le* TT covers the end point of SP, as shown in (295). The agent X will inevitably participate in the eventuality during TT. The APCC thus predicts that the eventive reading of *-le* will force the realization of the agent. By contrast, for the stative reading, TT locates within TP, so that the actions of X are not covered by TT. As a result, the APCC requires the absence of the agent. Both these predictions are correct, as shown in (293) and (294).

The difference between the patterns of *anzhuang* 'install' and *hua* 'draw' lies in whether the eventive reading is compatible with agent omission, and as I have shown, the deeper reason for the difference is that the presence/absence of the delegation event leads to different results from the APCC.

We have not yet seen how the LoC counterparts of (288/289) and (293/294) behave. We may hope that they also pattern with their canonically ordered counterparts, just like the 1-phase verbs do. However, this does not seem to be the case unfortunately.

(297) Qiang shang (ganggang/ xianzai) anzhuang le kongtiao.
     wall on   just now   now   install   ASP air-conditioner
     i) 'On the wall was installed an air-conditioner (just now).'
     ii) 'On the wall is installed an air-conditioner (now).'

(298) Zhi   shang (*ganggang/ xianzai) hua le xiangrikui.
      paper on   just now   now   draw ASP sunflower
      i) 'On the paper sunflowers are drawn (now).'
      ii) 'On the paper someone drew sunflowers (just now).'

(299) Qiang shang Zhangsan (ganggang/ xianzai) anzhuang le kongtiao.
      wall on   Zhangsan just now   now   install   ASP air-conditioner
      i) 'On the wall Zhangsan installed an air-conditioner (just now).'
      ii) 'On the wall there is an air-conditioner installed by Zhangsan (now).'

(300) Zhi   shang Zhangsan (ganggang/ xianzai) hua le xiangrikui.
      paper on   Zhangsan just now   now   draw ASP sunflower
      i) 'On the paper Zhangsan drew sunflowers.'
      ii) 'On the paper there are sunflowers drawn by Zhangsan (now).'

4.3 Accounting for the Data with the APCC

The felicitous stative reading found in (299) and (300) is unexpected. The APCC predicts that an agent cannot be realized at all in the stative alignments, regardless of whether there is a delegation event or not. Although this prediction is borne out for the canonically ordered sentences, it is not in the case of LoC. The stative reading of (299) and (300) is thus unaccounted for.

One potential way to account for them is to hypothesise that the LoC structure contains a (high) stativizer. Michaelis (2011) defines stativization as 'a linguistic procedure through which the speaker creates a stative predication from one whose lexical verb or argument array, or both, requires a dynamic construal (1361)'. As for the stativization of an accomplishment such as *anzhuang* 'install' (which Kratzer (2000) categorizes as a target state verb), Kratzer (2000) suggests that this results from a zero affix which existentially quantifies over the event variable. The output of this process is a stative predicate. Since an agent is allowed in the eventive reading in LoC (also shown in (299) and (300)), the grammaticality of the stative reading in (299) and (300) can be understood if stativization applies quite late in a LoC. On this view, the agent remains in (299) and (300) because stativization occurs after the attachment of the external argument. If we adopt this analysis, then (299) and (300) can be accounted for without challenging the APCC. Since by hypothesis this stativizer is only introduced in LoC, there is no mechanism that can stativize the eventive reading of (289) and (293), and therefore these will lack a stative reading, as required.

The stativizer story may create a minor problem to the patterns displayed by -*zhe* LoC, though. The stativizer suggests that the stative reading of LoC will allow an agent as long as the eventive reading of LoC allows an agent, since the former is stativized from the latter. As I have shown in Chapter 3, the eventive reading of LoC with an agent is accepted marginally by some native speakers but not all, while the stative reading of -*zhe* LoC does not allow an agent at all (see (208)). Both the behaviours are correctly captured by the APCC, but if we assume that the same stativizer also exists in the case of -*zhe* LoC, then the stative reading of -*zhe* LoC with an agent is expected to be also marginally accepted like its eventive counterpart is, which is unfortunately not the case. The stativizer account thus still faces problems and may need further investigations.

So far, I have investigated both 2-phase verbs allowing delegation and disallowing delegation, but there is a third pattern that is different from these two, represented by *kai* 'open'. As discussed in Sect. 3.3.3.2, transitive 'open' in Chinese can be interpreted as involving either a causation relation or a maintenance relation, which leads to three possible mental models. This makes the case a complicated one.

When I discussed the case of *kai* 'open' in the previous chapter, I suggested that its become event is an instantaneous change-of-state (which is an achievement, see Sect. 3.3.3.2) and so contains only an initial point and an end point. Since the verb is incompatible with the delegation context, in the causation case, its mental model only contains the causing event e_1, the instantaneous become event e_2 and the result state e_s. Depending on how long e_1 lasts, there are two possible mental models: e_2 may overlap with the end point of e_1, or follow the end point of e_1 and of course does not overlap with it. The two situations are shown in (301) and (302) respectively.

(301)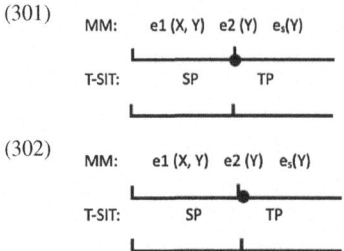

(302)

(301) represents the scenario in which the agent kept making an action on the door until it opened, while (302) represents the scenario where the agent performed an action (such as shooting a ball onto the door or pressing a button that controls an electronic door), and the door opened after the completion of the action. If we add TT to the alignments in (301) and (302), we will see how the APCC predicts the grammaticality of the relevant examples in the two scenarios.

(303)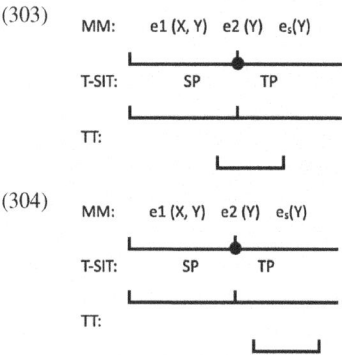

(304)

(303) and (304) show the eventive reading and the stative reading of the overlapping case. e_2 overlaps with the end point of e_1, and they also mark the end point of SP. Therefore, as long as TT covers the end point of SP as required by eventive -*le*, the agent X will have to participate during TT, so the APCC predicts that the agent has to be realized. Contrastively, in the stative reading, TT is located in TP and does not overlap with the time of e_1 at all. The APCC thus predicts that the agent must be omitted in the stative reading. The predictions are correct, as shown in (305) and (306). The eventive reading of (306) is marked by a hashtag rather than a star because the reading is unavailable in this scenario but possible in another, which I will show in the following part.

(305) Zhangsan (ganggang/ *xianzai) kai le men.
Zhangsan just now now open ASP door
'Zhangsan opened the door (just now).'
Not: 'the door is opened (now) as a result of Zhangsan opened it.'

4.3 Accounting for the Data with the APCC   109

(306)   Men   (#ganggang/   xianzai)   kai   le.
        door   just now   now   open   ASP
        'The door is opened (now).'
        Not: 'the door was opened (just now).'

The non-overlapping scenario will be more easily understood with a certain context, such as one in which Zhangsan pressed a button and then the door opened. The eventive reading and the stative reading of this scenario are shown as follows. Different from the overlapping scenario, now we have two possible alignments for the eventive reading, represented in (307) and (308). When e_2 follows the end point of e_1, the end point of SP will align with e_2. Therefore, when TT is required to cover the end point of SP, it can overlap with e_1 (see (307)), or not overlap with it (see (308)). The agent X can thus either participate or not participate during TT, so that the APCC predicts that in the eventive reading of this scenario, agent omission is optional. The stative reading is similar to the stative reading of the other cases, as shown in (309), and the prediction of the APCC is still that agent omission is forced. These predictions are again correct, as the following examples indicate.

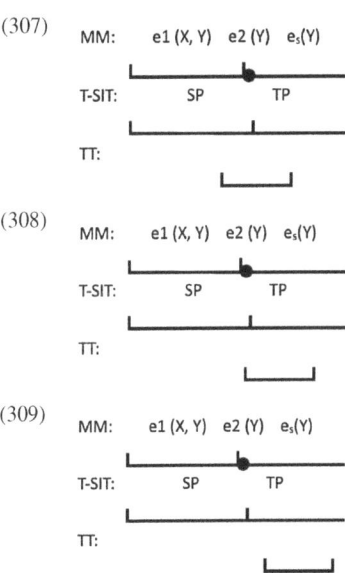

(310) Zhangsan (ganggang/ *xianzai) kai le men.
Zhangsan just now now open ASP door
'Zhangsan opened the door (just now).'
Not: 'The door is opened (now) as a result of Zhangsan opened it.'

(311) Men (ganggang/ xianzai) kai le.
door just now now open ASP
i) 'The door is opened (now).'
ii) 'The door was opened (just now).'

What differentiates the non-overlapping scenario with the overlapping scenario is whether agent omission is allowed in the eventive reading. The modifier 'just now' in (311) is allowed in the context where Zhangsan pushed a button and then the door opened, but not in the context where Zhangsan kept pushing the door until it opened. This is also supported by (312), which is a natural continuation.

(312) Zhangsan yi an anniu, men kai le.
Zhangsan one push button door open ASP
'Zhangsan pushed the button and the door opened.'

This is reminiscent of the English example in (313) suggested by Rappaport Hovav and Levin (2012), which can also be represented by the alignment in (308), since the definition for the perfective aspect in English is also TT covering the end point of SP. The APCC thus correctly predicts the grammaticality of this example as well.

(313) Sally kept tugging on the door until it finally opened.
(Rappaport Hovav and Levin 2012, 23)

The causation relation represented by *kai* 'open' has been analysed, and now I will turn to the maintenance relation. This is the case in which the agent did not cause the state of the door to change from closed to open but rather made efforts to keep the door open. I looked into this case in Sect. 3.3.3.2, where I reviewed Kratzer's (2000) and Neeleman and van de Koot's (2012) discussion on this topic. I adopted Neeleman & van de Koot's definition for the maintenance relation:

(314) a. Maintenance is a relation between two eventualities: a maintaining state or event and a maintained state
b. Maintenance lacks a temporal dimension: the maintaining state or event must be contemporaneous with the maintained state.
c. Maintenance is counterfactual: if the maintaining state or event were absent, the maintained state would not exist either. (Neeleman and van de Koot 2012, 39)

As the definition suggests, the mental model of the maintenance relation of *kai* 'open' should only have one phase, in which the causing event and the lasting state occur

4.3 Accounting for the Data with the APCC   111

simultaneously. It is thus predicted that the stative reading is unavailable, since there is no result state with a presupposition for TT to anchor. This prediction is borne out, since when the examples with the maintenance interpretation are modified by 'now', the meaning becomes incomprehensible, which can be seen in (315) and (316).

(315) Zhangsan (*xianzai) kai le men.
      Zhangsan now open ASP door
(316) Men (#xianzai) kai le.
      door now open ASP

The eventive reading is represented in (317), which predicts that the agent must be projected. It is borne out, too, as shown in (318) and (319).

(317) MM: e1(X, Y) & e$_s$(Y)
             └──────┘
      T-SIT: SP
             └──────┘
      TT:
                └──────┘

(318) Zhangsan (ganggang) kai le men.
      Zhangsan just now open ASP door
      'Zhangsan kept the door open (just now).'
(319) #Men (ganggang) kai le.
      door just now open ASP
      Intended reading: 'the door was kept open (just now).'

Therefore, the APCC makes the correct predictions for all the situations found with the three cases of 2-phase verbs represented by 'install' 'draw' and 'open'. In the next section, I will review a paper that also aims to account for the agent omission phenomenon, discuss its drawbacks and show how the APCC does a better job in capturing the examples presented in the paper.

4.3.3 Evidence from the Pro Drop Cases

In Sect. 2.2, I argued that there can be some apparently agentless cases that result from pro drop + topicalization rather than agent omission, and such examples present a potential confound for the present study. I have shown in Sect. 2.2 how the two types of data can be differentiated, and in this section I am going to argue that the distribution of the pro drop cases also follows from and thus supports the APCC.

According to Neeleman and Szendrői (2007, 2008), in radical pro drop (also known as discourse pro drop), which is the pro drop type that the Chinese pro drop belongs to, the null argument (i.e., the pro) is a regular pronoun in syntax that fails to be spelled out at PF. This suggests that in Chinese, pro drop of an agent is expected to be impossible where the agent does not exist in syntax. Since the APCC makes predictions on whether an agent is allowed to be projected syntactically, under the assumption that the APCC is correct, we will expect that the pro drop cases display the following pattern: firstly, for a possible agentless pro drop case, its agentive counterpart is expected to be permitted by the APCC; in the meantime, the cases that are predicted by the APCC as obligatorily agentless (e.g., the stative reading of -*le*) are expected to never have a homophonous pro drop counterpart. In what follows, I will show both of these predictions are borne out, which suggests that the distribution of the pro drop cases also supports the APCC.

I have shown in (285) (repeated below as (320)) that the verb *da* 'hit' does not allow agent omission, which is correctly predicted by the APCC. However, with certain contexts, an example like (321) seems to be acceptable.

(320) *Lisi   da   le.
       Lisi   beat ASP
       Intended meaning: 'Lisi was/is beaten.'

(321) Haizi   da   le,   zuoye   hai   bu   xie,
       child   hit   ASP   homework   still not   write
       zenme   ban?
       how   do
       Lit: 'The child was beaten, and he was still reluctant to finish his homework. What could we do?'

I argue that (321) is resulted from pro drop and topicalization, since it can pass agentivity tests and cannot be an answer to non-topic question. As shown in (322), the example can be modified by the agent-oriented adverb 'violently'. Meanwhile, the example can only be used to answer the topic question (323) but not the non-topic question (324).

(322) Haizi   henhende   da   le,   zuoye   hai   bu   xie,
       child   violently   hit   ASP   homework   still not   write
       zenme   ban?
       how   do
       Lit: 'The child was beaten violently, and he was still reluctant to finish his homework. What could we do?'

(323) Haizi   zenmeyang   le?

4.3 Accounting for the Data with the APCC   113

	child	how		ASP	
	'How was the child?'				
(324)	Nabian	fasheng	le	shenme	shi?
	there	happen	ASP	what	thing
	'What happened there?'				

Therefore, we expect the agentive counterpart of this pro drop case to be allowed by the APCC, and this is borne out. As (325) (repeated from (286)) shows, the agent of (320) can be realised, and I have argued previously that this is correctly captured by the APCC.

(325)	Zhangsan	da	le	Lisi.
	Zhangsan	beat	ASP	Lisi
	'Zhangsan beat Lisi.'			

If the APCC is correct, we also expected that a sentence of which the agent is disallowed to be realised syntactically by the APCC never has a homophonous pro drop counterpart. One typical example is the stative reading of *-le*.

(326)	Kongtiao	xianzai	anzhuang	le.	
	air-conditioner	now	install	ASP	
	'The air-conditioner is installed now.'				
(327)	*Zhangsan	xianzai	anzhuang	le	kongtiao.
	Zhangsan	now	install	ASP	air-conditioner
	Intended: 'there is now an air-conditioner installed by Zhangsan.'				

I have shown that the pattern displayed in (326) and (327) is successfully accounted for by the APCC. Now the key point is whether it is true that (326) cannot have a homophonous pro drop counterpart. I have suggested in Sect. 2.2 that the way to detect whether a pro drop structure exists is through the agentivity tests, and the way to detect whether an agent omission structure exists is to check whether it can be an answer to non-topic questions. Therefore, if (326) does not pass agentivity tests, it will suggest that the pro drop counterpart does not exist, which is what we expected. This is borne out, too:

(328)	Kongtiao	xianzai	*(xinbuzaiyande)	anzhuang	le.
	air-conditioner	now	carelessly	install	ASP
	'The air-conditioner is installed now (*carelessly).'				

Similar to the stative reading of *-le*, the stative reading of *-zhe* is another example that is predicted by the APCC as obligatorily agentless, and it displays the same pattern.

(329) Kongtiao   (*xinbuzaiyande)   zai   qiang   shang
       air-conditioner carelessly   at   wall   on
       anzhuang   zhe
       install   ASP
       'An air-conditioner is installed on the wall (*carelessly).'

In sum, the distribution of the agentless pro drop cases suggests that the APCC makes correct predictions on whether an agent is allowed to be projected syntactically.

4.4 Tan's (1991) Passivisation Account of Agent Omission

The agent omission phenomenon in Mandarin Chinese has not drawn much attention in the literature. Li and Thompson (1994) and Li (2015) mention it in their works, but neither investigates the phenomenon in a systematic way. Tan's (1991) PhD thesis discusses this structure in more detail and proposes an account for it. One example of agent omission that Tan presents is as follow:

(330) Lisi   chai   le   najian   fangzi.
       Lisi   demolish   ASP   that-CL   house
       'Lisi demolished that house.'
(331) Najian   fangzi   chai   le.
       that-CL   house   demolish   ASP
       'That house was demolished.' (Tan 1991, 45)

Tan (1991) hypothesises several possible strategies to account for the absence of the agent in (331): middle construction, *tough* construction or passivisation. He applies diagnostics and rules out the first two strategies, and thus turns to the passivisation account. He suggests that although Mandarin has a passive form marked by *-bei*, example (331) represents another passive form that lacks a passive morpheme.

However, I argue that Tan's argument for treating the agentless cases as resulting from passivisation is not strong enough, because agent omission (expletivization) is also a potential account that needs to be considered. I have shown in Sect. 4.3.1, using agentivity tests, that the agents are completely eliminated rather than covertly present, and the tests receive the same result on (331), as shown in (332). Therefore, I argue against Tan's passivisation account and insist that (331) should also be considered an agent omission case.

4.4 Tan's (1991) Passivisation Account of Agent Omission

(332) a. Najian   fangzi   (*xinbuzaiyande/   *xinganqingyuande)
         that-CL   house   carelessly   willingly
         chai   le
         demolish   ASP
         i) 'That house was demolished (*carelessly/*willingly).'
         ii) 'That house is demolished (*carelessly/*willingly).'

    b. Najian   fangzi   (*yong   tuituji)   chai   le.
       that-CL   house   with   bulldozer demolish   ASP
       i) 'That house was demolished (*with a bulldozer).'
       ii) 'That house is demolished (*with a bulldozer).'

    c. (*Wei-le   ganjue   anquan,)   najian   fangzi   chai   le.
       in order to feel   safe   that-CL   house   demolish   ASP
       i) 'That house was demolished (*in order to feel safe).'
       ii) 'That house is demolished (*in order to feel safe).'

Tan (1991) further points out that the 'passivisation' is subject to some constraints, since there are verbs that have inconsistent passivisability when they combine with different objects. Tan gives the following examples to show this phenomenon:

(333) a. Wo   tan   le   najia   gangqin.
         I   play   ASP   that-CL   piano
         'I played that piano.'

    b. *Najia   gangqin   tan   le.
       that-CL   piano   play   ASP
       Intended reading: 'that piano was played.'

(334) a. Wo   tan   le   nazhi   quzi.
         I   play   ASP   that-CL   concerto
         'I played that concerto.'

    b. Nazhi   quzi   tan   le.
       that-CL concerto   play   ASP
       'That concerto was played.'

(335) a. Wo   fang   le   fengzheng.
         I   play   ASP   kite
         'I played the kite.'

    b *Fengzheng   fang   le.
       kite   play   ASP
       Intended reading: 'the kite was flown.'

(336) a. Wo   fang   le   bianpao.
         I   play   ASP   firecrackers
         'I played the firecrackers.'

	b.	Bianpao	fang	le.
		firecrackers	play	ASP

'The firecrackers were played.' (Tan 1991, 78–79)

The examples above concern two different verbs, *tan* and *fang*, although they can both be translated as 'play' in English. (333) and (334) show that the agent can be absent when *tan* combines with 'concerto' but not with 'piano', while (335) and (336) indicate that the agentless variant is available only when *fang* combines with 'firecrackers', but not with 'kite'. Tan (1991) attributes this pattern to the telicity of the VP. He suggests that only VPs that have an ending point of time ([+EPOT]) are compatible with the passivisation he suggests. Since the ending point of 'concerto playing' is reached when the last note of the concerto is played, and the ending point of 'firecrackers playing' is the moment when the firecrackers are completely burnt, (334a) and (336a) are [+EPOT] and thus can be 'passivised'. In the meantime, 'piano playing' and 'kite playing' do not have a clear ending point, so (333a) and (335a) are [-EPOT], which cannot undergo the passivisation.

I argue that although the [±EPOT] account captures the contrast in (333)-(336), it faces some problems. Firstly, if [±EPOT] is responsible for the (un)grammaticality of (333b)-(336b), we should expect all the aspectual variants of them to show the same grammaticality, since telicity is independent from aspect, but this is not the case:

(337)	a.	Wo	zai	tan	najia	gangqin.
		I	ASP	play	that-CL	piano
		'I am playing that piano.'				
	b.	*Najia	gangqin	zai	tan.	
		that-CL	piano	ASP	play	
		Intended: 'that piano is being played.'				
(338)	a.	Wo	zai	tan	nazhi	quzi.
		I	ASP	play	that-CL	concerto
		'I am playing that concerto.'				
	b.	*Nazhi	quzi	zai	tan.	
		that-CL	concerto	ASP	play	
		Intended: 'that concerto is being played.'				
(339)	a.	Wo	zai	fang	fengzheng.	
		I	ASP	play	kite	
		'I am playing the kite.'				
	b.	*Fengzheng	zai	fang		
		kite	ASP	play		
		Intended: 'the kite is being flown.'				

4.4 Tan's (1991) Passivisation Account of Agent Omission

(340) a. Wo   zai   fang   bianpao.
           I   ASP   play   firecrackers
           'I am playing the firecrackers.'
       b. Bianpao   zai   fang
           firecrackers ASP   play
           'The firecrackers are being played.'

Since 'concerto playing' is [+EPOT], both (334b) and (338b) are expected to be good on Tan's account. However, (338b) is unexpectedly infelicitous. The same VP shows different compatibility with different aspectual markers, suggesting that whether an agentless variant is permitted is at least not only determined by telicity.

I argue that the patterns shown above can all be captured by the APCC. The four VPs are associated with three different types of mental model. For 'piano playing' and 'kite playing', the mental model is simple: since the VPs do not allow a delegation context, it only contains an activity e_1. When these two VPs combine with -le or -zai, the alignments are as in (341) and (342), respectively. Since the VPs are 1-phase, only the eventive reading of -le is available. In either case, the agent X must participate in the interval of TT. As a result, the APCC predicts that the agent must be projected. This is attested in (333b), (335b), (337b) and (339b). Therefore, Tan (1991) is on the right track in suggesting the (333b) and (335b) are bad because they are [-EPOT], but the deeper reason is that (333b) and (335b) are not allowed with an eventive reading because they do not permit delegation, and they cannot have a stative reading because they are [-EPOT] and thus have no result states.

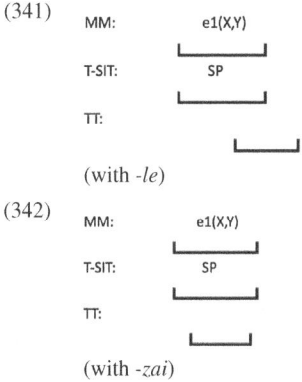

(341) MM: $e_1(X,Y)$
      T-SIT: SP
      TT:
      (with -le)

(342) MM: $e_1(X,Y)$
      T-SIT: SP
      TT:
      (with -zai)

The mental model of 'firecrackers playing' is more complex. It contains an event e_1 that is the agent lighting the firecrackers, an event e_2 that is the firecrackers burning, where the agent is definitely not participating, and e_s representing the result state of the firecrackers. Since it is a 2-phase VP, we need to consider both the eventive reading and the stative reading yielded by -le. (336a) and (336b) only show that the two examples are acceptable, but do not specify whether it is the eventive reading or the stative reading that is acceptable, or both. I thus test it with the temporal modifiers:

(343) a. Wo   (ganggang/   *xianzai)   fang   le   bianpao.
         I   just now   now   play   ASP   firecrackers
         'I played the firecrackers (just now).'
         Not: 'there are (now) firecrackers played by me.'

     b. Bianpao   (ganggang/   xianzai)   fang   le.
        firecrackers just now   now   play   ASP
        i) 'The firecrackers were played (just now).'
        ii) 'The firecrackers are played (now).'

The test shows that when the agent is realized, only the eventive reading is available. Contrastively, when the agent is absent, both readings are possible. The alignments representing the readings of 'firecrackers playing' combining with -le are shown in (344), (345) and (346).

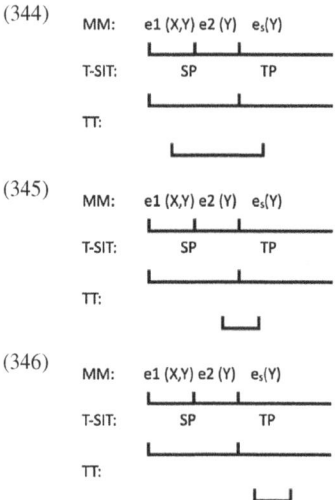

If we consider (344) and (345) together, we can see that the APCC predicts that the eventive reading allows the agent to be either projected or omitted. Depending on how long TT stretches, e_1 may or may not overlap with TT. Therefore, the agent X may or may not participate during TT. This optionality is attested, since the modifier 'just now' is compatible in both (343a) and (343b). (346) shows that, similar to almost all the stative -le cases discussed in this chapter, the position of TT makes the overlap between e_1 and TT impossible, and no agent is thus permitted in the stative reading. This is also borne out in (343a) and (343b).

The case with -zai is simpler. (347) and (348) represent the agentive case and the agentless case respectively, and the APCC predicts that with -zai, the agent can be present or absent. This prediction is also correct, as shown in (340a/b).

4.4 Tan's (1991) Passivisation Account of Agent Omission   119

(347)

(348)

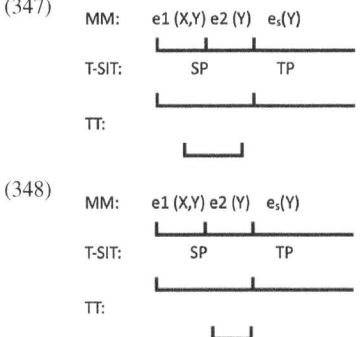

Now we come to the case of 'concerto playing', where Tan's [±EPOT] account faces a problem, as reflected in (334b) and (338b). 'Concerto playing' is an incremental theme VP, which ends when the last note of the concerto has been played on the piano. Here I assume that incremental theme verbs generally have a result state (which should not be confused with the perfect state associated with any completed event), and the result state in this case is that the concerto has been completely played and appreciated by the audience, which makes the concerto somehow regarded as affected. The VP does not allow the delegation context either, so no e_D should be considered in the mental model. The mental model thus contains the playing event e_1 during which the agent participates, the become event e_2 which denotes that the concerto is gradually completed note by note on the piano, and the result state e_s that the concerto is finished by the pianist. e_1 and e_2 take place simultaneously. Since the verb is 2-phased, we need to consider both the eventive reading and the stative reading of *-le*. (349) shows the case of eventive *-le*, (350) of the stative *-le* and (351) of *-zai*. The APCC predicts through the alignments in (351) that the combination of *-zai* and 'concerto playing' will force the presence of the agent, which is borne out in (338a/b).

(349)

(350)

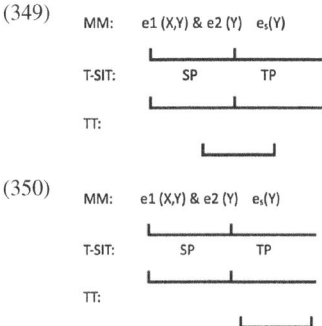

(351)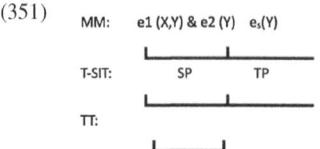

(334a/b) only show that -*le* is compatible but does not specify the grammaticality of the eventive reading and the stative reading. I thus use the temporal modifier test again:

(352) a. Wo   (ganggang/ *xianzai)   tan   le   nazhi   quzi.
           I   just now   now   play   ASP   that-CL   concerto
      'I played the concerto (just now).'
      Not: 'the concerto is played (now) because I played it.'
   b. Nazhi   quzi   (*ganggang/ xianzai)   tan   le.
      that-CL   concerto   just now   now   play   ASP
      i) 'The concerto was played (just now).'
      ii) 'The concerto is played (now).'

(352a/b) show the same pattern with *hua* 'draw' discussed in Sect. 3.3.2: the eventive reading requires the projection of the agent while the stative reading requires the omission of it. This is not surprising if we see the alignments in (349) and (350). In the eventive reading, TT covers the end point of SP, and the agent X must participate during TT; in the stative reading, TT positions itself within TP, and there is no way for the agent X to participate in TT. Therefore, the APCC successfully captures the contrast between (334b) and (338b), which Tan's (1991) account fails to do. Moreover, the (un)grammaticality of (333)–(340) are all correctly predicted by the APCC.

The second issue that Tan's proposal faces is that some [-EPOT] VPs also allow agent omission, such as (276), repeated as (353). This is not expected on Tan's account but can be easily captured by the APCC. As I have suggested, since 'cake baking' involves delegation, its mental model contains the event of delegation e_D, which causes the APCC to be met, as shown in (354).

(353) Dangao   (ganggang/ *xianzai)   kao   le.
      cake   just now   now   bake   ASP
      'A cake was baked just now.'
      Not: 'a cake is baked now.'

(354)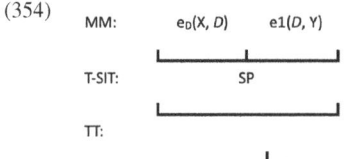

Furthermore, Tan (1991) makes a connection between passivisation and telicity, but conceptually speaking, it is unclear why passivisation is impacted by telicity, so Tan's account is more descriptive than explanatory. I argue that whether an agent is projected or eliminated is determined by whether it participates in the eventualities during the aspectual interval, which explains the relation between agent projection/omission and aspect in Mandarin Chinese in a deeper manner.

4.5 The Difference Between Stative *-zhe* and Stative *-le*

In the previous chapter and this chapter, I have investigated *-zhe* and *-le* respectively, and the stative uses of the two markers exhibit some similarities. Therefore, it is important to compare them and discuss how they differ from one another.

The interchangeability of stative *-zhe* and stative *-le* has been discussed in the literature. Hu (1995) and Djamouri and Paul (2017) propose that *-le* requires a CoS presupposition, and based on their proposal, I further suggested in the previous chapter that although *-zhe* does not require such a presupposition, it is not incompatible with it. This can be seen when the two markers combine with a verb that necessarily contains a prior activity, such as *anzhuang* 'install'. Its compatibility with *-zhe* shows that *-zhe* does not require the absence of such a prior activity.

(355) Qiang shang xianzai anzhuang zhe/le kongtiao.
wall on now install ASP air-conditioner
'On the wall is installed an air-conditioner now.'

In the APCC account, although stative *-zhe* aligns TT within TP while stative *-le* makes TT cover the CoS presupposition that is found everywhere in a result state, when combining with a 2-phased VP and obtaining a stative reading, the alignments happen to be exactly the same, as shown in (356). It is thus unsurprising that *-le* and *-zhe* are interchangeable in (355). Therefore, stative *-le* and *-zhe* are expected to behave the same way when interacting with modifiers. However, as Djamouri and Paul (2017) point out, some modifiers are compatible with *-le* but not *-zhe*, as shown in (357).

(356) T-SIT: SP   TP
              └────┴──────
       TT:
                    └────┘

(357) a. Qiang   shang   (*yijing/   anzhuang   zhe   yitai   kongtiao.
                         *zaojiu/
                         *you)
         wall   on   already/   install   ASP   1-CL   air-conditioner
                         long.since/
                         again
         'On the wall is installed an air-conditioner.'
      b. Qiang   shang   (yijing/   anzhuang   le   yitai   kongtiao.
                         zaojiu/
                         you)
         wall   on   already/   install   ASP   1-CL   air-conditioner
                         long.since/
                         again
         'On the wall has (already/long since/again) been installed an air-conditioner.'

The examples above show that in an agentless *-zhe* sentence like (357a), the CoS presupposition seems to be compatible but inaccessible for modifiers. Contrastively, *-le* does not exhibit this restriction. This suggests that perhaps *-zhe* blocks the projection of the CoS presupposition in some way.

I argue that one potential solution is to hypothesise that *-zhe* takes the CoS presupposition as an input but does not output it. As a result, the CoS presupposition cannot project past *-zhe* and thus cannot be modified by anything attaching to it on a higher projection. This will explain why verbs with such a presupposition are not incompatible with *-zhe*, but cannot be modified anymore on the presupposition of the event after they combine with *-zhe*. In the meantime, *-le* does not block the output, and the modification is thus fine, as shown in (357b). In some sense, *-zhe* can be seen as a stativizer as it suppresses the projection of the CoS presupposition. Arguably, this hypothesis provides a coherent characterisation of the difference between *-zhe* and stative *-le*.

4.6 Conclusion

In this chapter, I have investigated the presence/absence of external arguments in sentences marked with *-le*, including canonically ordered structures and LoC structures. I showed through agentivity tests that the absent external arguments are completely eliminated rather than covertly present. Therefore, the agentless *-le* sentences should be treated as resulting from agent omission.

I showed that the aspectual marker *-le* can yield either an eventive reading or a stative reading, and proposed a definition for *-le* that unifies these two functions: *-le* covers a bound, and whether *-le* yields the eventive reading or the stative reading depends on whether the bound is the end point of SP or the presupposition of a prior change-of-state event. Based on the definitions of eventive *-le* and stative *-le*, I applied the APCC to a range of examples and showed that it makes correct predictions to all the patterns found, with only one exception, which is that *-le* LoC with an agent can unexpectedly receive a stative reading. I attributed this exception to an additional stativizing mechanism operative in LoC but not in canonically ordered sentences. In Chapter 2, I have shown that some certain agentless cases should be attributed to pro drop + topicalization rather than agent omission but suggested that the two types of cases can be differentiated through tests. In this chapter, I further show that the distribution of the pro drop cases marked by *-le* is in favour of the APCC. I also reviewed Tan's (1991) account of agentless *-le* sentences and argued that it cannot capture the patterns found with the aspectual variants of the *-le* examples, which however could be accounted for successfully by the APCC. Finally, I compared stative *-le* with stative *-zhe*, which are sometimes treated as semantically interchangeable in the literature. I argued that their difference lies in that stative *-zhe* takes the change-of-state presupposition as an input but blocks its output, while stative *-le* does not block it. This can explain why stative *-le* and stative *-zhe* behave differently when modified by adverbials oriented on the presupposition.

References

Bhatt, R. 2009. Structural properties of implicit arguments. Paper presented at the University of Massachusetts at Amherst, Semantics Seminar.

Bhatt, J., and D. Embick. 2017. Causative derivations in Hindi-Urdu. *Indian Linguistics* 78 (1–2): 93–151.

Djamouri, R., and W. Paul. 2017. A new approach to-zhe in Mandarin Chinese. In *Studies in Japanese and Korean historical and theoretical linguistics and beyond*, 110–123. Leiden: Brill.

Hu, W. 1995. Verbal semantics of the presentative sentences. *Yuyanyanjiu* 2: 100–111.

Klein, W., P. Li, and H. Hendriks. 2000. Aspect and assertion in Mandarin Chinese. *Natural Language & Linguistic Theory* 18 (4): 723–770.

Kratzer, A. 2000. Building statives. Paper presented at the Annual Meeting of the Berkeley Linguistics Society.

Lasnik, H. 1988. Subjects and the θ-criterion. *Natural Language & Linguistic Theory* 6 (1): 1–17.

Li, C. 2015. Event structure and argument realization. *SKY Journal of Linguistics*: 28.

Li, C.N., and S.A. Thompson. 1989. *Mandarin Chinese: A functional reference grammar*. Berkeley and Los Angeles: University of California Press.

Li, C.N. & S.A. Thompson. 1994. On 'middle voice'verbs in Mandarin. *Voice: Form and function* 27: 231.

Lin, J. 2003. Temporal reference in Mandarin Chinese. *Journal of East Asian Linguistics* 12: 259–311.

Michaelis, L.A. 2011. Stative by construction. *Linguistics* 49 (6): 1359–1399.

Neeleman, A., and K. Szendrői. 2007. Radical pro-drop and the morphology of pronouns. *Linguistic Inquiry* 38: 671–714.

Neeleman, A., and K. Szendrői. 2008. Case morphology and radical pro-drop. In *The limits of syntactic variation*, ed. Biberauer Theresa, 331–348. Amsterdam & Philadelphia: John Benjamins.
Neeleman, A., and H. van de Koot. 2012. The linguistic expression of causation. In *The theta system: Argument structure at the interface*, 37. Oxford: Oxford University Press.
Pan, H. 1996. Imperfective aspect zhe, agent deletion, and locative inversion in Mandarin Chinese. *Natural Language and Linguistic Theory*, 14 (2): 409–432. https://doi.org/10.1007/bf00133688
Paul, W., Y. Lu, and T.H.-T. Lee. 2019. Existential and locative constructions in Mandarin Chinese. *The Linguistic Review* 37 (2): 231–267.
Rappaport Hovav, M., and B. Levin. 2012. Lexicon uniformity and the causative alternation. In *The Theta system: Argument structure at the interface*, 150–176. Oxford: Oxford University Press.
Ross, C. 1995. Temporal and aspectual reference in Mandarin Chinese. *Journal of Chinese Linguistics* 23: 87–135.
Shi, Z. 1990. Decomposition of perfectivity and inchoativity and the meaning of the Particle Le in Mandarin Chinese. *Journal of Chinese Linguistics* 18: 95–123.
Smith, C. 1997. The aspectual system of Mandarin Chinese. In *The parameter of aspect*, 263–294. Berlin: Springer.
Sybesma, R. 1997. Why Chinese verb-le is a resultative predicate. *Journal of East Asian Linguistics* 6 (3): 215–261.
Tan, F. 1991. Notion of subject in Chinese. Doctoral dissertation. Stanford University.
Tham. S.W. 2012. Result in Mandarin verb compounds. *Proceedings of Sinn und Bedeutung* 16 (2): 599–612.
Williams, E.S. 1974. *Rule ordering in syntax*. Doctoral Dissertation. Massachusetts Institute of Technology.
Williams, E.S. 1985. PRO and subject of NP. *Natural Language & Linguistic Theory* 3 (3): 297–315.

Open Access This chapter is licensed under the terms of the Creative Commons Attribution-NonCommercial-NoDerivatives 4.0 International License (http://creativecommons.org/licenses/by-nc-nd/4.0/), which permits any noncommercial use, sharing, distribution and reproduction in any medium or format, as long as you give appropriate credit to the original author(s) and the source, provide a link to the Creative Commons license and indicate if you modified the licensed material. You do not have permission under this license to share adapted material derived from this chapter or parts of it.

The images or other third party material in this chapter are included in the chapter's Creative Commons license, unless indicated otherwise in a credit line to the material. If material is not included in the chapter's Creative Commons license and your intended use is not permitted by statutory regulation or exceeds the permitted use, you will need to obtain permission directly from the copyright holder.

Chapter 5
Agent Omission with *-guo*

Abstract This chapter begins with the proposal of an updated definition for the aspectual marker *-guo* that covers the several functions found with it, which is supported by further evidence. Based on the relevant temporal relation yielded by the definition, the APCC again successfully captures all the agent omission cases marked by *-guo*.

Keywords Discontinuity · Aspectual marker *-guo*

5.1 Introduction

After the investigation of agent omission in sentences with the aspectual markers *-zai*, *-zhe* and *-le*, there is only one aspectual marker left in Mandarin, which is *-guo*. *-guo* has been generally treated as a perfective marker in the literature. In particular, it has been taken to mark an event as having been experienced or a state as no longer in existence (see Chao 1968; Li and Thompson 1989; Iljic 1990; Smith 1997; Klein et al. 2000; Xiao and McEnery 2004; Li 2011 among others).

Li (2011) concludes from the literature that *-guo* reveals three different functions when combining with verbs in different situation types: 'experiential' with atelic verbs, 'ex-habitual' with states and 'deresultative' with telic verbs. I argue that these three functions can be further unified into one, which is that *-guo* marks that an eventuality in the event structure of the verb was the case once but has discontinued later.

Then a new question arises: which eventuality is marked by *-guo* as discontinued if the event structure contains more than one eventuality (i.e., an event with a resultant state)? The facts indicate that in some cases either option is available, but in other cases, there are some restrictions at play, which appear correlated with the presence/absence of the external argument. For example, (358) is compatible with the discontinuity of either the installing event or the installed state, while (359) disallows the interpretation that the event has discontinued while the result state still holds.

(358) Zhangsan   anzhuang   guo   zhetai   kongtiao.
      Zhangsan   install   ASP   this-CL   air-conditioner
      'Zhangsan has installed this air-conditioner before (it may or may not have been uninstalled)'

(359) Zhetai   kongtiao   anzhuang   guo.
      this-CL   air-conditioner install   ASP
      'The air-conditioner has been once installed (but it has been uninstalled)'

In what follows, I will again account for the data marked by *-guo* with the hypothesised APCC. In preparation for the analysis, I propose a novel definition of *-guo* under Klein et al.'s (2000) aspectual system as in (360) and adduce evidence to show why this definition outshines its potential alternatives.

(360) *-guo*   TT in a phase of T-SIT and has a presupposition that the phase it covers has discontinued.

I will show that the APCC makes accurate predictions across the board, with only one exception, which is that the interpretation that the installing event has discontinued in (359) is unexpectedly unacceptable. However, I argue that this exception should be attributed to pragmatics, and I will demonstrate that this interpretation is in fact allowed on the grammatical level. If this is correct, then the APCC makes the correct predictions across the board.

I have organised this chapter as follows: Sect. 5.2 discusses how *-guo* should receive a unified definition that covers the various functions proposed in the literature, and how this definition should be formulated in Klein et al. (2000)'s aspectual system. 5.3 applies the APCC to account for the data with *-guo*. Section 5.4 concludes the chapter.

5.2 The Definition of *-guo*

The aspectual marker *-guo* has been widely investigated in the literature. It is mostly regarded as a 'perfective' or 'experiential' marker. Li and Thompson (1989) suggest that *-guo* marks that an event has been experienced, which, in other words, has occurred at least once. For instance, (361) expresses that 'I' have eaten Japanese food at least once.

(361) Wo   chi   guo   riben   fan.
       I   eat   ASP   Japanese   food
       'I've eaten Japanese food (before).'
                                        (Li and Thompson 1989, 226)

5.2 The Definition of -*guo*

Li and Thompson (1989) also point out that in a sentence marked by -*guo*, such as (362), not only the event has been experienced, but also the result state is already over. (362) entails that a visit to China took place last year but the visitor is not in China anymore. Li and Thompson (1989) suggest that this 'not in China anymore' interpretation is not surprising because 'if something has been experienced, it is over' (Li and Thompson 1989, 229).

(362) Ta   qunian   dao   zhongguo   qu   guo.
      3sg   last.year   to   China   go   ASP
      'S/He had been to China last year.'

                                              (Li and Thompson
                                              1989, 226)

Smith (1997) regards -*guo* as conveying a perfective viewpoint. She proposes that -*guo* 'presents a prior closed situation of any type and conveys that its final state no longer obtains' (Smith 1997, 266). This definition also accounts for (362), as its final state has discontinued. For examples such as (361), in which the VP is atelic and thus does not have a non-transitory final state, Smith (1997) indicates that 'any discontinuity posited holds only vacuously' for them (Smith 1997, 267).

Klein et al. (2000) investigate the correlati3.2.2on between telicity and the definition of -*guo* in a more detailed manner. They hold the view that -*guo* requires the topic time (TT) to locate after the last phase of the situation time (T-SIT) of the VP.[1] Therefore, a one-phase (atelic) verb marked by -*guo* denotes that the only phase is in the past time, while a two-phase (telic) verb marked by -*guo* entails that the second phase (i.e., the result state) is in the past and thus no longer holds.

Li (2011) reviews the various proposals on -*guo* and concludes that -*guo* has three functions depending on what type of verbs it combines with, as shown in (230).

(363) | Situation type (with -*guo*) | Typical function |
      |---|---|
      | Atelic events | 'Experiential' |
      | Stative verbs | 'Ex-habitual' |
      | Telic events | 'Deresultative' |

The three types of verbs with -*guo* are exemplified as (364), (365) and (366), respectively. When -*guo* combines with an activity such as 'studying judo', the sentence has an experience interpretation that 'I' have the experience of studying judo at least once, and the studying event, of course, took place in the past and then terminated or finished. When -*guo* combines with a state like in (365), it denotes an 'ex-habitual'

---

[1] Similar to what I did in Sect. 3.2.2, I have again simplified the definition and omitted the notion of the Distinguished Phase (DP) in Klein et al.'s (2000) work. Please see the footnote under Sect. 3.2.2 for more details.

state (Li 2011, 28), suggesting that the state of owing a debt was once true but then no longer holds. Because of this function of *-guo*, it can hardly combine with non-reversible state such as 'old' or 'dead' (Li and Thompson 1989).

(364) Wo   xue   guo   roudao.
      I   study   ASP   judo
      'I have studied judo before.'

(365) Wangping   qian   guo   wo   yibi   zhang.
      Wangling   owe   ASP   I   one-CL   debt
      'Wangping has owed me a debt (and no longer does).'

(366) Zhege   pingzi   dapo   guo
      this-CL   vase   hit-break ASP
      'This vase has once broken (but it has been repaired).' (Li 2011, 27–28)

The combination of *-guo* and telic verbs seems to be more complicated. As shown in (366), when *-guo* combines with telic events such as the resultative verbal compound *dapo* 'break' (literally 'hit-break'), it marks discontinuity of the broken state, which is a deresultative interpretation. (366) thus appears to entail that the broken state of the vase was then reversed.

However, (366) is an apparently agentless sentence, and if we also consider its transitive counterpart, the pattern becomes interestingly different. Li (2011) points out that when the agent is projected, the discontinuity of the result state is not forced any more, as illustrated in (367):

(367) Lisi   dapo   guo   zhege   pingzi.
      Lisi   hit-break ASP   this-CL   vase
      'Lisi has broken this vase before (it may or may not have been repaired).'

(Li 2011, 28)

(367) only suggests that the 'hit-break' event took place in the past but is unspecified about whether the result state of the vase was then reversed or not, which, in a sense, shares some similarities with the case of (364). Although Smith (1997) and Klein et al. (2000) take telicity into consideration when defining *-guo*, the pattern shown in (366) and (367) cannot be captured by their proposals. This pattern suggests that the presence/absence of the agent may somehow impact which function *-guo* reveals.

It should be noted, however, that the 'hit-break' examples are different from the other example because the predicate is a resultative verb compound (RVC) rather than a simplex verb. Whether external argument omission in RVCs and that in simplex verbs are the same phenomenon is still under exploration (which I will discuss in a more detailed way in Chapter 6), and in the following discussion I will only focus on simplex verbs. In the data analysis of the previous chapters, I have used *anzhuang* 'install' as a representative example of a telic verb, and as a simplex verb, it exhibits the same pattern.

(368) Zhetai   kongtiao   anzhuang   guo.
      this-CL   air-conditioner install   ASP
      'The air-conditioner has been once installed (but it has been uninstalled)'
(369) Zhangsan anzhuang   guo   zhetai   kongtiao.
      Zhangsan install   ASP   this-CL   air-conditioner
      'Zhangsan has installed this air-conditioner before (it may or may not have been uninstalled)'

I argue that the three functions of *-guo* identified by Li (2011) can be unified into one. Consider the event structures of the verbs that belong to different situation types: atelic events only contain one event, and when *-guo* combines with it, it denotes that this event has terminated or finished; stative verbs have only a state in their event structure, and *-guo* claims that this state was once the case and then does not hold anymore; telic verbs consist of an activity and a result state, and the examples show that the both the interpretation that the activity terminated or finished and the interpretation that the result state no longer holds are possible. It then seems natural to suggest that *-guo* marks that an eventuality in the event structure of the verb was once true but no longer is.

The next question is when *-guo* marks the discontinuity of an event and when it marks that of a state. If the verb is atelic, its event structure only contains an event; and if the verb is stative, its event structure only contains a state. In these two cases, of course *-guo* does not have a choice. When combining with telic verbs, both the event and the result state seem to be available to be marked by *-guo*. But as shown in the contrasts in (366)/(367) and (368)/(369), the choice is not completely free and seems correlated with the projection of the agent, so what restriction it is subject to becomes the next intriguing question.

I will discuss in Sect. 5.3 that the patterns shown in (366)/(367) and (368)/(369) have some differences although they appear to be similar, and I will argue that there are both syntactic and pragmatic restrictions on these patterns, with the syntactic restriction attributed to the APCC. I will also show that the absence/presence of external arguments in the full set of *-guo* examples can be accounted for by the APCC.

Again, before attempting to capture the data with the APCC, a definition for *-guo* under Klein et al.'s (2000) aspectual system needs to be determined. I have shown above that *-guo* marks the discontinuation of an eventuality in the event structure of the verb, and the eventuality can be either an event or a state, depending on the verb type. Therefore, the definition of TT must guarantee this discontinuity.

There are three potential accounts. The first one is Klein et al.'s (2000) proposal: TT falls in the post-time of the target phase. Therefore, *-guo* indicates that the target phase is in the past. This proposal can account for the cases of (364), (365), (366) and (368), but not (367) and (369), since they obtain an interpretation that it is the source phase rather than the target phase that is in the past. We may adjust this proposal and suggest that *-guo* requires TT to be in the post-time of a phase of T-SIT, so it can also capture (367) and (369). I will analyse this revised account later with the other two potential accounts.

The second account is that TT covers the end point of a phase of T-SIT. Since it covers the end point, it will guarantee that the phase has terminated. Finally, a third option is to hypothesise that TT stays in a phase of T-SIT and comes with a presupposition that the phase it covers has discontinued. On this account, the discontinuation interpretation of -*guo* is guaranteed by the presupposition.

It is not straightforwardly clear which account is better, but I argue that structures involving modification with temporal adverbials allow us to choose. In the previous chapter, I discussed the data with -*le*, and the following examples with -*le* suggests that in Mandarin Chinese a temporal modifier like 'yesterday' or 'now' always denotes the time of the interval covered by TT.

(370) Kongtiao   zuotian   anzhuang   le.
      air-conditioner yesterday   install   ASP
      'The air-conditioner was installed yesterday.'

(371) Kongtiao   xianzai   anzhuang   le.
      air-conditioner now   install   ASP
      'The air-conditioner is installed now.'

(372)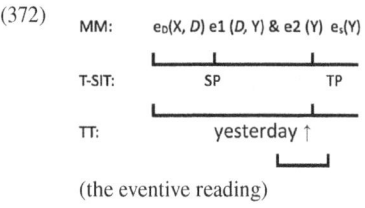

(the eventive reading)

(373)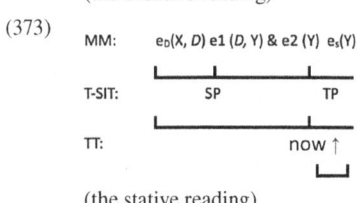

(the stative reading)

(370) is represented in (372). If the installing event lasted for a few days and finished yesterday, it can be described with (370). However, if the event took place since the day before yesterday and finished just now, (370) does not sound proper. This suggests that the modifier 'yesterday' must denote the end point of SP that TT marks, rather than a random point in SP that it covers. In (371), as represented in (373), TT covers an interval in TP, and 'now' marks a point in this interval.

5.2 The Definition of -*guo*   131

Therefore, if we assume that TT follows a phase of T-SIT or TT covers the end point of a phase of T-SIT, then a temporal modifier in (368) is predicted to denote the time after the state terminated or exactly the moment that the state terminated (i.e., the time the change of state happened). However, as the translation of (374) indicates, this is an incorrect prediction. The temporal modifier 'ten years ago' marks a point in TP instead.

(374) Zhetai   kongtiao   shi   nian   qian   anzhuang   guo.
       this-CL   air-conditioner   ten   year   before   install   ASP
       'The air-conditioner was in the installed state ten years ago.'
       Not: 'the air-conditioner was in the uninstalled state ten years ago'
       and not: 'the air-conditioner was uninstalled by someone ten years ago.'

Such modification data can be accounted for, however, if we adopt the presupposition proposal. If TT aligns within TP and at the same time presupposes that TP has terminated, it is expected that 'ten years ago' marks a point of TP, since it is covered by TT, as shown in (375).[2]

(375)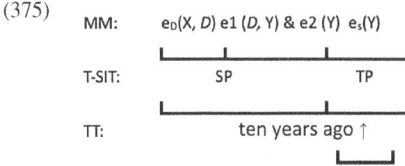

Similarly, when the transitive counterpart of (374) is modified by 'ten years ago', the post-time account and the end point account will predict that ten years ago, Zhangsan had already finished installing the air-conditioner, so the installing event might take place eleven years ago. Meanwhile, the presupposition account will predict that ten years ago is the time the installing event occurred. The translation of (376) shows that the presupposition account makes the correct prediction again.

---

[2] This proposal also allows TT to align in SP, so an SP termination reading will be obtained and 'ten years ago' will be predicted to denote the time of SP. I have not shown this reading in the translation of (374) because it sounds unavailable when the example is uttered out of the blue. However, I argue that this is due to a pragmatic factor, and given proper context the reading will become available. See the discussions below (408)/(409). If 'ten years ago' is inserted in (409), it will denote the time the air-conditioner was installed (i.e., the time of SP).

(376) | Zhangsan | shi | nian | qian | anzhuang | guo | zhetai | kongtiao.
Zhangsan | ten | year | before | install | ASP | this-CL | air-conditioner

'Zhangsan installed this air-conditioner ten years ago.'
Not: 'Zhangsan has already finished installing this air-conditioner ten years ago.'

Therefore, I will define *-guo* as in (377). Interestingly, its alignment is similar to that of *-zhe*, except that *-guo* has an additional presupposition that guarantees the discontinuation.

(377)   *-guo*   TT in a single phase of T-SIT and has a presupposition that the phase it covers has discontinued.

5.3 Accounting for the Data with the APCC

In the following part, I will investigate the patterns of the presence/absence of agents in the combination of different verb types and *-guo*. Similar to the previous chapters, I will align the mental model of the verb, T-SIT and TT and consider what predictions the APCC makes based on these alignments and whether they are borne out.

As usual, before approaching the analysis part, agentivity tests need to be applied to guarantee that the data with *-guo* do not have covert agents and thus should receive the agent omission account. I hereby adduce again the three pieces of evidence that I have used in the previous chapters, as shown in (378).

5.3 Accounting for the Data with the APCC   133

(378) a. Zhetai   kongtiao   (*xinbuzaiyande/   *xinganqingyuande)
          this-CL   air-conditioner   carelessly   willingly
          anzhuang   guo.
          install   ASP
          'This air-conditioner was once in an installed state (*carelessly/*willingly).'

     b. Zhetai   kongtiao   (*yong   luosidao)   anzhuang   guo.
         this-CL   air-conditioner   with   screwdriver   install   ASP
         'This air-conditioner was once in an installed state (*with a screwdriver).'

     c. (*Wei-le   ganjue   nuanhuo,)   zhetai   kongtiao   anzhuang   guo.
         in order to feel   warm   this-CL   air-conditioner install   ASP
         'This air-conditioner was once in an installed state (*in order to feel warm).'

As the results of these tests indicate, the agents in the apparently agentless sentences marked by -*guo* are eliminated thoroughly and thus should be subject to the APCC.

5.3.1 1-Phase Verbs

The first type under discussion is activities incompatible with delegation, of which the mental model only contains the event e_1 that completely overlaps with SP. Since TT stays in SP, the external argument X must participate in the event during TT. The APCC thus predicts that the external argument must be lexicalised. As (380) and (381) show, the predictions are correct.

(379)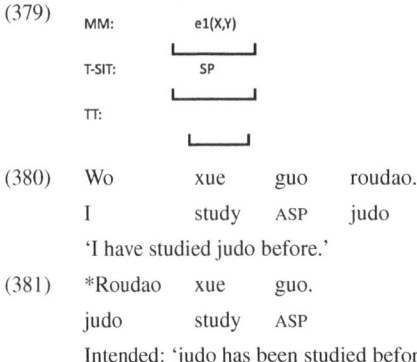

(380) Wo   xue   guo   roudao.
      I   study   ASP   judo
      'I have studied judo before.'

(381) *Roudao xue   guo.
       judo   study ASP
       Intended: 'judo has been studied before.'

When an activity is compatible with the delegation context, its mental model will additionally contain a delegation event e_D that precedes e_1. SP aligns with the sum of e_D and e_1. Therefore, when TT locates in SP, it may or may not overlap with e_D in which the external argument X participates, depending on the size of TT, as shown in (382) and (383). Therefore, the APCC predicts that the external argument can be optionally omitted, and no matter whether the agent is present, the sentences always obtain the SP termination reading, since SP is the only phase available. This type of VPs is represented by 'baking a cake', and (384) and (385) corroborate the prediction.

(382)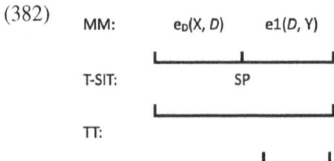

(383) MM: $e_0(X, D)$ $e_1(D, Y)$
       T-SIT: SP
       TT:

(384) Wo   kao   guo   zhege   dangao.
       I   bake   ASP   this-CL   cake
       'I have baked this cake.'

(385) Zhege   dangao   kao   guo.
       this-CL   cake   bake   ASP
       'This cake has been baked.'

1-phase verbs also include states. Stative verbs only contains a state in their event structure, and they do not allow the delegation context, so the mental model of states only have a state, which aligns with SP. Similar to (379), the agent X will inevitably participate in the state during TT, so the APCC predicts that the external argument must be projected. This is corroborated by (387) and (388).

(386) MM: $e_s(X, Y)$
       T-SIT: SP
       TT:

(387) Wangping   qian   guo   wo   yibi   zhang.
       Wangling   owe   ASP   I   one-CL   debt
       'Wangping has owed me a debt (and no longer does).'

(388) *Yibi   zhang   qian   guo.
       one-CL   debt   owe   ASP
       Intended meaning: 'a debt has been owed (and no longer does).'

5.3.2 2-phase Verbs

2-phase verbs also vary in their compatibility with the delegation context. Among the 2-phase verbs that disallows delegation, there are different types that need to be discussed separately, since the mental models they can have vary. I will discuss two types of VPs represented by *die* 'fold' and *kai* 'open' and investigate the mental models they are compatible with.

(389)   Lisi   die   guo   zhechuang   beizi
        Lisi   fold   ASP   this-CL   quilt
        'Lisi has folded this quilt before (it may or may not have been unfolded).'

(390)   Zhechuang   beizi   die   guo.
        this-CL   quilt   fold   ASP
        'This quilt has once been folded (but it has been unfolded).'

The mental model of the VP 'fold the quilt' has a causing event e_1 and a simultaneous become event e_2, followed by the result state. T-SIT consists of SP, which aligns with e_1 and e_2, and TP, which aligns with the result state e_s. According to the definition of *-guo*, TT can locate in either SP or TP. When it is in SP, it will yield the SP termination reading, while if it is in TP, the TP termination reading will be obtained. In the former case, the agent X will have to participate in the interval of TT, while in the latter case, the agent X will never have such a chance. As a result, the APCC predicts that in the SP termination reading, the external argument must be lexicalised, while in the TP termination reading, the external argument must be eliminated. Therefore, it is predicted that (389) must not specifically require the broken state to be reversed, while (390) must do.

(391)

(392)

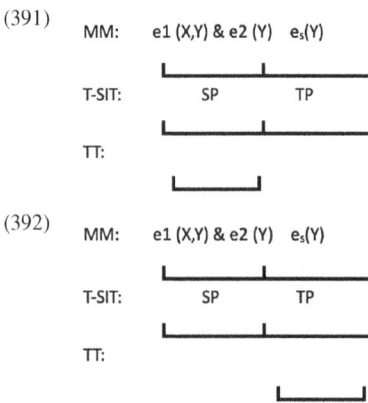

Note that the unavailability of the SP termination reading in (390) can be easily verified, as (390) is not acceptable if the quilt has never been unfolded; however, whether the TP termination reading is unavailable in (389) may not be as straightforward, since the example is NOT incompatible with a situation that the quilt was unfolded after being folded. I argue that the temporal modifier test can be applied again to show that this reading is truly ruled out:

5.3 Accounting for the Data with the APCC 137

(393) Lisi   shi   tian   qian   die   guo   zhechuang   beizi
      Lisi   ten   day   before fold   ASP   this-CL   quilt
      'Lisi folded this vase ten days ago (it may or may not have been unfolded).'
      Not: 'this quilt was in a folded state ten days ago because Lisi folded it (but it has been unfolded).'

If the TP termination reading existed in (389), (393) would be expected to be compatible with a situation in which Lisi folded the quilt, say, eleven days ago and the quilt was in a folded state ten days ago and was unfolded nine days ago. However, this situation is not permitted, and 'ten days ago' must denote the time of Lisi's activity in (393). Therefore, I argue that the TP termination reading is indeed not allowed in (389), as correctly predicted by the APCC. Although I will not show it, this test can be applied to all the accomplishments in the following discussions with the same result.

Kai 'open' represents another type of 2-phase verbs that are incompatible with delegation. As I have discussed in the previous chapters, the VP 'opening a door' has several possible mental models that need to be analysed separately. It is possible for e_2 to either overlap with the end point of e_1 or follow e_1 immediately, but when 'open' combines with *-guo*, the APCC makes similar predictions in the two different mental models. The SP termination reading and the TP termination reading with the two possible mental models are shown as follows.

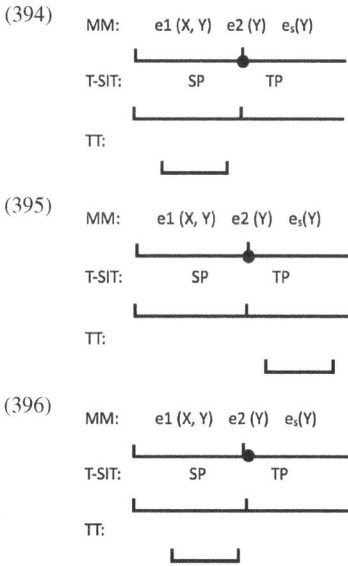

(394) MM: e1 (X, Y) e2 (Y) e$_s$(Y)
      T-SIT: SP   TP
      TT:

(395) MM: e1 (X, Y) e2 (Y) e$_s$(Y)
      T-SIT: SP   TP
      TT:

(396) MM: e1 (X, Y) e2 (Y) e$_s$(Y)
      T-SIT: SP   TP
      TT:

(397)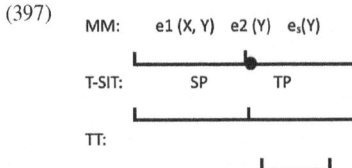

As the alignments show, the APCC predicts that in the SP termination reading, the external argument must be lexicalised, while in the TP termination reading, the external argument must be eliminated. Again, the predictions are borne out, as (398) and (399) corroborate.

(398) Zhangsan kai guo men.
Zhangsan open ASP door
'Zhangsan has opened this door (it may or may not have been closed).'
Not: 'this door was once open because Zhangsan opened it (but it has been closed).'

(399) Men kai guo.
door open ASP
'This door was once open (but it has been closed).'
Not: 'this door was once opened (it may or may not have been closed)'

What makes *kai* 'open' a special verb in this category is that it allows a third mental model that represents the maintenance relation, which I have investigated in the previous chapters. This mental model contains a maintaining event and a maintained state that occur simultaneously, which align with the only phase of T-SIT.

(400)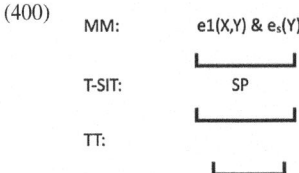

Since the agent X inevitably participates in the eventuality during TT, the APCC predicts that the agent must be present. This is confirmed by the data in (401) and (402). Therefore, the three different mental models of *kai* 'open' with *-guo* are all captured by the APCC.

5.3 Accounting for the Data with the APCC   139

(401) Zhangsan   kai   guo   men.
      Zhangsan   open   ASP   door
      'Zhangsan has kept this door open (it
      may or may not have been closed).'

(402) #Men   kai   guo.
      door   open   ASP
      Intended: 'this door was once kept open
      (it may or may not have been closed).'

So far, all the predictions made by the APCC are borne out. Now I will investigate the case of accomplishments compatible with delegation, whose mental model is the most complex. Since the delegation context is allowed, the mental model has the delegation event e_D, followed by the causing event e_1 and the simultaneous become event e_2, which in turn is followed by the result state e_s. SP covers e_D, e_1 and e_2, while TP aligns with e_s. Therefore, as shown in the diagrams, in the SP termination reading, the external argument X may or may not participate during TT (see (403) and (404)), while in the TP termination reading, X can never do so (see (405)).

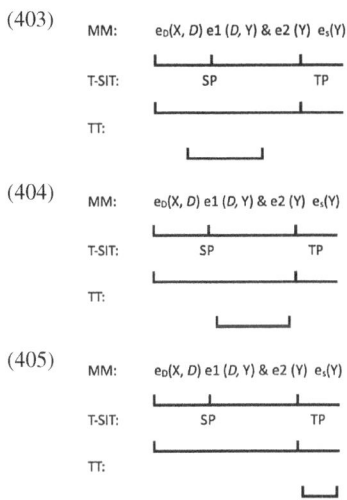

The APCC thus predicts that in the SP termination reading, the external argument is optionally projected, while in the TP termination reading, the external argument must be eliminated.

(406) Zhetai   kongtiao   anzhuang   guo.
      this-CL   air-conditioner install   ASP

'This air-conditioner was in the installed state (but it has been uninstalled)'
Not: 'this air-conditioner was installed by someone (it may or may not have been uninstalled).'

(407) Zhangsan   anzhuang   guo   zhetai   kongtiao.
      Zhangsan   install   ASP   this-CL   air-conditioner
      'Zhangsan has installed this air-conditioner before (it may or may not have been uninstalled)'

All the predictions of the APCC are confirmed by the data, with the exception of the unavailable SP termination interpretation of (406). As (404) shows, (406) is expected to be compatible with the reading that the installing event has finished and the air-conditioner can be still in the installed state, but this reading seems hard to be obtained.

Nevertheless, I argue that the surprising absence of this reading is likely due to pragmatics rather than syntax, and the reading can be obtained given proper context. Consider the following situation:

Imagine that Zhangsan's job is installing air-conditioners, and Lisi can consult a system that records whether a certain air-conditioner has been installed or not yet. Now Zhangsan has the identification number of an air-conditioner, but he does not know whether he has installed this one or not. They had a conversation like this:

(408) Zhangsan: Ni   bang   wo   cha   cha,
                   you   help   I   check   check
                   zhetai   kongtiao   anzhuang   guo   ma?
                   this-CL air-conditioner   install   ASP   Q.mark
                   'Please help me check it. Has this air-conditioner been installed?'

(409) Lisi: Zhetai   kongtiao   anzhuang   guo.
                   this-CL   air-conditioner   install   ASP
                   'This air-conditioner has been installed.'

(409) is identical to (406), but in the context provided, it obtains the SP termination interpretation. This suggests that the APCC still makes the right prediction in this case, and that the reading is missing in (406) due to some pragmatic factor.

My account for this pragmatic restriction is as follow. When (406) is uttered out of the blue, it is understood as (405) but not (404) by default, and this is because in the most common context where people utter (406), namely looking at an air-conditioner and talking about it, (405) communicates new information while (404) does not. When one looks at an air-conditioner that is not installed, it is possible that they cannot tell whether it is a brand new one or it had been installed somewhere and was then uninstalled, and (405) can let them know that it is not a brand new one, which is new information. But if one looks at an installed air-conditioner, they will know immediately that there was an installing event in the past. Since what (404) communicates is simply 'the air-conditioner was installed', it does not give any new

5.3 Accounting for the Data with the APCC   141

information to the listener, so it is generally considered improper. Contrastively, (408) and (409) make the alignment in (404) acceptable because when Zhangsan asked about the air-conditioner, he could not see the state of it. Instead, he only had an identification number, so it makes sense to ask whether there was an installing event in the past or not. And it is also understandable why (407) is not influenced by pragmatics in the same way that (406) is: even if one knows the existence of a previous installing event once they see an installed air-conditioner, that Zhangsan was the person who installed the air-conditioner is still meaningful new information.

It should be noted that this context cannot rescue the unavailable SP termination reading in sentences such as (390), repeated as (410).

(410) Zhechuang   beizi   die   guo.
       this-CL   quilt   fold   ASP
       'This quilt has once been in folded state
       (but it has been unfolded).'
       Not: 'this quilt was once folded by
       someone (it may or may not have been
       unfolded)'

Even if we imagine that someone has a job that is to fold quilts, the following conversation still sounds odd. The interpretation that the quilt was then unfolded cannot be cancelled.

(411) Zhangsan: #Ni   bang   wo   cha   cha,
                  you   help   I   check   check
                  zhechuang beizi   die   guo   ma?
                  this-CL   quilt   fold   ASP   Q.mark
                  Intended: 'please help me check it. Has this quilt been
                  folded?'
(412) Lisi: #Zhechuang beizi   die   guo.
                  this-CL   quilt   fold   ASP
                  Intended: 'this quilt has been folded.'

The contrast suggests that the unavailable reading of (410) is correctly ruled out by the APCC as the verb does not allow a delegation context, while the seemingly unavailable reading of (406) is allowed by the APCC but ruled out by pragmatic reasons unless an appropriate context is provided. The APCC thus successfully captures all the data with *-guo* that I have investigated above.

5.3.3 Evidence from the Pro Drop Cases

In Sect. 4.3.3, I argued that the distribution of the agentless pro drop cases provides further support for the APCC. This conclusion was mainly based on two observations:

firstly, the agentive counterpart of an agentless pro drop case is always allowed by the APCC; secondly, the cases that are predicted by the APCC as obligatorily agentless are not found with a homophonous pro drop counterpart. I have shown in Sect. 4.3.3 that the agentless pro drop cases marked by *-le* follow these lines. In this section, I will show that the cases marked by *-guo* show the same distribution and again support the APCC.

In the previous section, I have shown that 'studying judo' displays the following pattern when marker by *-guo*, which is correctly accounted for by the APCC. However, although (414) is ill-formed on its own, with certain contexts, its acceptability can be significantly improved, as exemplified in (415):

(413) Wo xue guo roudao.
 I study ASP judo
 'I have studied judo before.'

(414) *Roudao xue guo.
 judo study ASP
 Intended: 'judo has been studied before.'

(415) a. Q: xuyao hui roudao de ren,
 Women
 we need know judo SUB person
 roudao ni xue guo ma?
 judo you study ASP Q.mark
 'We need a person who knows judo. Judo, have you ever studied?'
 b. A: xue guo.
 Roudao
 judo study ASP
 'Judo, I have studied.'

I argue that (415b) is a result of pro drop + topicalization. (415b) can be an answer to (415a), which is a topic question, but it cannot answer a non-topic question such as (416):

(416) ni xue guo shenme?
 you study ASP what
 'What have you studied?'

Moreover, with the context of (415), (415b) can be modified by agent-oriented adverbs such as 'carefully' (note that this is unavailable without the context):

(417) Roudao renzhende xue guo.
 judo carefully study ASP
 'Judo, I have studied carefully.'

Therefore, (415b) is a pro drop case. Since its agentive counterpart (413) is felicitous and is captured by the APCC, it suggests that the first observation that supports the APCC is also found in cases marked by *-guo*.

The second observation from the *-le* cases that supports the APCC is that the cases predicted by the APCC as obligatorily agentless never have a homophonous pro drop counterpart. This is also the case with the examples marked by *-guo*. I have suggested above that the TP termination reading of *-guo* disallows an agent, which is captured by the APCC. Take (418) as an example again. Our prediction will be that it does not have a pro drop counterpart, which means it is incompatible with agentivity tests, which is borne out again as shown in (419).

(418)   Zhechuang   beizi   die   guo.
        this-CL   quilt   fold   ASP
        'This quilt has once been in folded state (but it has been unfolded).'

(419)   Zhechuang   beizi   (*renzhende)   die   guo.
        this-CL   quilt   carefully   fold   ASP
        'This quilt has once been in folded state (*carefully) (but it has been unfolded).'

Therefore, the agentless pro drop cases marked by *-guo*, just as their counterparts marked by *-le*, show a distribution that is in support of the APCC.

5.4 Conclusion

This chapter has focused on when the external arguments in sentences marked by *-guo* can be present or absent. I reviewed the definitions of *-guo* in the literature and argued that the proposed functions of *-guo* can be unified: *-guo* marks that an eventuality in the event structure of the verb was true but has then discontinued. As for how this unified function can be represented in Klein et al.'s (2000) aspectual system, I proposed that *-guo* requires TT to locate in a phase of T-SIT and that it introduces the presupposition that the phase it covers has discontinued. I adduced evidence from temporal modifiers to support this analysis.

Based on this proposed definition of *-guo*, I applied the APCC to the full range of data marked by *-guo*, and showed that the APCC makes the correct predictions for all the investigated cases, except for one, of which the unacceptability is not expected by the APCC. However, I argued that this exception should be attributed to pragmatics, and as long as a proper context is given, the case will be felicitous as the APCC predicts. The APCC thus successfully captures the full set of data marked by *-guo*, as it does to the examples marked by the other three aspectual markers discussed in the previous chapters. The distribution of the pro drop cases marked by *-guo* also goes along with the predictions that the APCC makes.

References

Chao, Y.R. 1968. *A grammar of spoken Chinese*. Berkeley: University of California Press.
Iljic, R. 1990. The verbal suffix -guo in Mandarin Chinese and the notion of recurrence. *Lingua* 81: 301–326.
Klein, W., P. Li, and H. Hendriks. 2000. Aspect and assertion in Mandarin Chinese. *Natural Language & Linguistic Theory* 18 (4): 723–770.
Li, D.C. 2011. 'Perfective paradox': A cross-linguistic study of the aspectual functions of -guo in Mandarin Chinese. *Chinese Language and Discourse* 2 (1): 23–57.
Li, C.N., and S.A. Thompson. 1989. *Mandarin Chinese: A functional reference grammar*. Berkeley and Los Angeles: University of California Press.
Smith, C. 1997. The aspectual system of Mandarin Chinese. In *The parameter of aspect*, 263–294. Berlin: Springer.
Xiao, R., and T. McEnery. 2004. *Aspect in Mandarin Chinese*. Amsterdam/Philadelphia: John Benjamins.

Open Access This chapter is licensed under the terms of the Creative Commons Attribution-NonCommercial-NoDerivatives 4.0 International License (http://creativecommons.org/licenses/by-nc-nd/4.0/), which permits any noncommercial use, sharing, distribution and reproduction in any medium or format, as long as you give appropriate credit to the original author(s) and the source, provide a link to the Creative Commons license and indicate if you modified the licensed material. You do not have permission under this license to share adapted material derived from this chapter or parts of it.

The images or other third party material in this chapter are included in the chapter's Creative Commons license, unless indicated otherwise in a credit line to the material. If material is not included in the chapter's Creative Commons license and your intended use is not permitted by statutory regulation or exceeds the permitted use, you will need to obtain permission directly from the copyright holder.

Chapter 6
Concluding Remarks

Abstract The final chapter concludes the whole book and brief reviews a few unsolved questions, including what languages could belong to the same camp with Mandarin in terms of the M parameter, and whether the missing agents in other Chinese structures such as resultative verb compounds should also be treated as agent omission and accounted for by the APCC.

Keywords APCC · Limitations and future directions

In this final chapter, I will give a brief review of the hypotheses I have proposed in this monograph and how they can account for the Mandarin Chinese data. I will also discuss the unsolved problems, which may motivate further investigations.

This monograph proposes two core hypotheses to account for the external argument omission phenomenon in Mandarin Chinese, which attempts to answer two questions: (i) cross-linguistically why the agents can be omitted in Mandarin Chinese but not in many other languages, and (ii) within the Chinese language when the omission is allowed and when it is disallowed. The first hypothesis, the M parameter, aims to explain why Mandarin Chinese allows [+m] external arguments to be expletivized when the UEAC indicates that such an operation is expected to be prohibited cross-linguistically. The M parameter hypothesises that languages like Chinese do not encode the requirement for a [+m] external argument syntactically in the predicates, while the languages with the other setting, such as English, do. I suggest that the UEAC, although a cross-linguistically constraint indeed, only applies to languages in the latter camp but not to Chinese. The hypothesis of the M parameter accounts for why Chinese is more lenient in allowing external argument omission than numerous other languages at the very beginning, but within the Chinese language there is still some rule for the omission to be explored. For what this rule is, I have proposed the second hypothesis: The Aspectual Proper Containment Condition (APCC). The APCC links the presence/absence of an external argument to aspect: it says that an external argument must be eliminated if and only if it is not an event participant during the interval specified by aspect. The APCC successfully captures the different patterns a predicate displays when it combines with different aspectual markers, confirming that the projection of the external argument is not only determined by the verb itself, but is also sensitive to aspect.

It must be admitted that although the two hypotheses can account for numerous cases of external argument omission in Chinese, the scale of this study has limitations. For example, due to the tentative nature of this study, it covers a small set of examples rather than conducting a large-scale study to test the hypotheses. Moreover, the study has investigated the four aspectual markers in Mandarin Chinese, but there are also some particular cases such as zero marker or multi-markers. Due to the time limit, the monograph has not thoroughly gone through all the possibilities, which is left for future study. Apart from these limitations, there are also two main unsolved questions, which can potentially lead to further explorations.

The first question is about the M parameter: since we assume that whether the [+m] requirement for the external argument is encoded syntactically in the predicate is a parameter, it is expected that there are other languages that have the same setting with Chinese, just as English has the same setting with languages such as Dutch, German and Greek. Unfortunately, due to the limit of time, I have not yet found many languages that belong to the Chinese camp. That said, Hindi-Urdu could be a potential member of the camp, as I have discussed in Sect. 2.4.

(420) a. peṛ   kaṭ   rahe   hẼ
         trees.M cut   Prog.MPI   be.Prs.Pl
         Lit: 'trees are cutting.' (i.e., trees are being cut.)
     b. kampani   peṛ   kaaṭ   rahii   hai
         company.f tree   cut   Prog.f   be.Prs
         'The company is cutting trees.'   (Bhatt and Embick 2017, 106)

Hindi-Urdu may be similar with Chinese in allowing agent omission, and we thus may wonder whether the data can also be accounted for in a similar way. Unfortunately, I have not had enough time to investigate this topic, and that I am not a speaker of the language even makes this task more difficult. Therefore, I will leave it for other people's studies in the future.

Another unsolved question concerns the external argument omission phenomenon found in resultative verb compounds (RVC) in Chinese. The RVC structure has been discussed widely in the literature. It consists of two verbal morphemes that are in a causal relation, with the former one representing a causing eventuality (henceforth V1) and the latter one representing a resulting eventuality (henceforth V2) (Huang et al. 2009). The RVC structure has been mentioned once in my previous analysis, where I cited Li's (2011) examples when investigating the -*guo* cases (see Sect. 5.2). The examples are repeated as below:

(421) Lisi   dapo   guo   zhege   pingzi
      Lisi   hit-break   ASP   this-CL   vase
      'Lisi has broken this vase before (it may or may not have been repaired).'

(422) zhege   pingzi   dapo   guo
      this-CL   vase   hit-break   ASP
      'This vase has once broken (but it has been repaired).'
      (Li 2011, 28)

The examples above seem to behave exactly the same with the simplex verb case *die* 'fold' that I have discussed in Sect. 5.3.4.1, so we will hope to account for the RVC examples in the same way with the APCC. Nevertheless, it is too early to do so before we can establish that the external argument omission in RVCs is identical to that found with simplex verbs, and there is presumably some evidence suggesting that it is not necessarily the case. For example, as Nishiyama (1998) points out, some Japanese V-V compounds (JVVCs) force the agent of V1 to be missing, although the first verb can never undergo agent omission when used separately:

(423) coat   ga   ki-kuzure   ta
      coat   -Nom   wear-get.out.of.shape   -Past
      'The coat was worn and got out of shape.'

(424) *John   ga   coat   o   ki-kuzure   ta
      John   -Nom   coat   -Acc   wear-get.out.of.shape -Past
      Intended meaning: 'John wore the coat and it got out of shape.'
      (Nishiyama 1998, 189)

(425) *coat   ga   ki   ta
      coat   -Nom   wear   -Past
      Intended meaning: 'the coat was worn.'

(426) John   ga   coat   o   ki   ta
      John   -Nom   coat   -Acc   wear   -Past
      'John wore the coat.'

Although (423) appears to be a case of agent omission, it can also be captured by other accounts. Nishiyama (1998) hypothesises that there is a phrase Tr(ansitivity)P that is higher than VP, and it is the active Tr that assigns the external argument. The JVVC is headed by V2, which is unaccusative in (423) and (424), so it is selected by inactive Tr rather than active Tr. As a result, the external argument of *ki* 'wear' is not omitted, but never assigned.

It is not be impossible to also account for the Chinese RVCs in a similar way, since some patterns displayed by RVCs are close to that of the JVVCs. For instance, unergatives can occur as V1 in an RVC that is compatible with a missing agent (see (427)), and as I have discussed in Sect. 3.3.3.1, unergatives on their own do not permit agent omission by nature. If the external argument of *ku* 'cry' here is also considered as not exist at the very beginning, then we are not dealing with a case of agent omission at all, and it is thus groundless to apply the APCC.

(427) shoupa ku shi le
handkerchief cry wet ASP
'Someone cried with the handkerchief so it got wet.'

(428) Zhangsan ku shi le shoupa
Zhangsan cry wet ASP handkerchief
'Zhangsan cried with the handkerchief and got it wet.'

Therefore, although my hope is that the absent external argument in RVCs can also be captured by the APCC (and some examples may look promising), more researches are needed to establish its eligibility. Due to the time constraints, I cannot investigate this issue in the present study and thus leave it to future research.

References

Bhatt, J., and D. Embick. 2017. Causative derivations in Hindi-Urdu. *Indian Linguistics* 78 (1–2): 93–151.
Huang, C.T.J., Y.H.A. Li, and Y. Li. 2009. *The syntax of Chinese*. Cambridge: Cambridge University Press.
Li, D.C. 2011. 'Perfective paradox': A cross-linguistic study of the aspectual functions of-guo in Mandarin Chinese. *Chinese Language and Discourse* 2 (1): 23–57.
Nishiyama, K. 1998. V-V compounds as serialization. *Journal of East Asian Linguistics* 7: 175–217.

Open Access This chapter is licensed under the terms of the Creative Commons Attribution-NonCommercial-NoDerivatives 4.0 International License (http://creativecommons.org/licenses/by-nc-nd/4.0/), which permits any noncommercial use, sharing, distribution and reproduction in any medium or format, as long as you give appropriate credit to the original author(s) and the source, provide a link to the Creative Commons license and indicate if you modified the licensed material. You do not have permission under this license to share adapted material derived from this chapter or parts of it.

The images or other third party material in this chapter are included in the chapter's Creative Commons license, unless indicated otherwise in a credit line to the material. If material is not included in the chapter's Creative Commons license and your intended use is not permitted by statutory regulation or exceeds the permitted use, you will need to obtain permission directly from the copyright holder.

The manufacturer's authorised representative in the EU is Springer Nature Customer Service Centre GmbH, Europaplatz 3, 69115 Heidelberg, Germany. If you have any concerns regarding our products, please contact ProductSafety@springernature.com

Printed and bound by CPI Group (UK) Ltd, Croydon, CR0 4YY